HUMOR
IS WHERE YOU FIND IT

Look No Further

By

Taylor Reese

AAcorn Books
Micaville, NC

Cover concept by Linda Murray
Cover Design by Morris Publishing
Book Design by Linda Murray

Published by:

AAcorn Books
P.O. Box 647
Micaville, NC 28755

ISBN: 0-9663666-0-3
Library of Congress Catalog Card Number: 98-71020

Printed in the USA by

MP

MORRIS PUBLISHING

3212 East Highway 30 • Kearney, NE 68847 • 1-800-650-7888

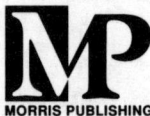

This book is
dedicated
to all readers
but
especially those who like
diversity in humorous subject matter.

Other books by Taylor Reese
written with co-author Jack R. Pyle

RAISING WITH THE MOON - The Complete Guide To
Gardening - and Living - by the Signs of the Moon.

YOU AND THE MAN IN THE MOON - The Complete
Guide to Using the Almanac

Foreword

Just as the kaleidoscope reveals a new display with every twist, so does life: endless patterns with each turn.

This eclectic collection of humor encompasses personal experiences, gossip, hearsay, and in some instances a laugh at the ironies that would otherwise become serious episodes as we travel our own private roads.

The definition of "humor" I like best is, "...the mental faculty of discovering, expressing, or appreciating the ludicrous or absurdly incongruous." The humor herein reaches toward that goal.

"Essay" is defined as "... an analytic or interpretive literary composition usually dealing with its subject from a limited or personal point of view." The varied humorous essays fit that description.

"Story" is defined, in one part, as a "...fictional narrative shorter than a novel." It is here where humor plays with the reader's imagination.

*

I totally subscribe to a comment William Allen White made on his 90th birthday: "Tell the people for me I enjoyed yesterday; I love today, and I am not afraid of tomorrow."

i

Special Appreciation:

To Jack R. Pyle, for his encouragement throughout all stages in the making of this book.

To Cousins Elizabeth, Margaret and Frances, whose constant goodwill and appreciation for humor spurred me to seek the highest in life, including a heightened sense of seeing humor in almost every facet of day-to-day living.

.

CONTENTS

iv

Good Night, Reuben

A friend was traveling by Greyhound bus from Miami to Charlotte during the night hours. Although against policy, she boarded carrying a tiny White Crowned Blue Amazon parrot, cleverly caged in a small reed container. She placed it inside her carry-on bag, with the top open, and placed the bag on the unoccupied seat beside her.

The bird was fully grown and knew many words. Later, the occupants of the bus were beginning to stop reading, talking, and beginning their nighttime naps. My friend placed a cloth napkin over the top of the cage.

That was Reuben's signal to be heard. He squawked, "Good night."

At this point the lady sitting across the aisle looked over at my friend and said, "Good night."

Within minutes Reuben again said, "Good night." The lady looked over, this time with a puzzled expression.

My friend, embarrassed, said, "Please excuse me, but I am an amateur ventriloquist, and I'm just practicing."

"Oh, how nice," said the lady, and then the three of them were quiet for the rest of the night.

When morning came and the occupants were beginning to talk, Reuben was once again heard from: "Good morning," he squawked, and the woman across the aisle looked over at my friend and said, "Good morning," and then added, "You know, I hope you keep at it, because you're really getting good."

Reuben remained quiet for the remainder of the trip, and has never again had the opportunity to help his owner with her ventriloquism.

1

His Honor's Ruling No. 1

After finding the defendant guilty of stealing a box of chocolates, the judge asked him if he had anything to say.

"Yes, Your Honor, I do. I didn't steal that candy for myself. I took it for a young woman and her child sitting just outside the door of the store. They looked pitiful and hungry."

"You did, huh?"

"Yes, sir, I did, Judge. I guess you could just call me a modern-day Robin Hood."

"Well, Robin Hood," said the judge, "I'll tell you what I'm going to do. I'm going to send you away to Sherwood Forest for three days.

"Next case."

The Gingerbread Man

Mama was a good woman and a great cook. One of her specialties was making gingerbread. We loved it. She would make all shapes and sizes, but we especially liked the "gingerbread man." It was always dark and gingery.

It was one of those gingerbread men that she used, hoping to help ensnare a wife for my bachelor uncle. Uncle Hobson was 38 and still single. The other uncles and aunts on my mother's side had married, and most of them had children. But not Uncle Hobson; he said women had their place and time, and that he never was at the right place at the right time.

Anyway, Uncle Hobson had to put up with a lot of teasing, urging, and subtle manipulation about being single at 38. The family thought that "Miss Ada," a spinster, was a perfect catch for him.

She, too, was about that age, and she had a brand new automobile.

Miss Ada was my first-grade teacher. She was one of those women with long hair, which she wrapped around in a bun and fastened it to the back of her head. I don't know how it stayed there, but it did. Sometimes it looked so big and bundlesome that it would almost make her head slant upward. In fact, when she was reprimanding us in class and shaking her head, the bun would bounce up and down, separately, it seemed, from her head. We used to cup our mouths as we quietly giggled.

"Take this gingerbread man to Miss Ada," my mother said. It fitted perfectly in one of her old handkerchief boxes, about 10 inches square. She had wrapped it in nice pink and white paper, tied a lavender ribbon diagonally across the box. "Be careful now; don't shake it or drop it. If you do, it will break."

"I'll be careful, Mama. But why are you doing this?"

"Never mind. You just take it and tell her that your mother sent it and hopes she likes it."

"You mean I can't give it to her and say it's from me?"

"All right," my mother said, "if you want to. Just tell her I made it for you to give to her."

The school bus came around the bend; I got on, holding my school bag in one hand and the handkerchief box in the other.

"What's that?" several of my schoolmates asked. I wouldn't tell them. I just said, "Nothing, it's for Miss Ada."

"Oh, he's got a gift for the teacher, he's got a gift for the teacher," they said. "He's her pet."

Just before they rang the bell for class to begin, I stepped up to Miss Ada's desk, handed her the box and said, "Miss Ada, my mother made this for you and said she hopes you will like it. It's from me, too."

"That's mighty sweet of your mother," she said, "and nice of you to bring it."

Then I looked her straight in the face and asked, "Did you and my Uncle Hobson have a date this past weekend?"

"Ramoth, that's none of your business. It's time for class. Go sit down."

During the day I felt I should have been granted special privileges. After all, I did bring her the gingerbread man. No one else had brought anything.

Later in the day I exercised what I thought was my right. I made a spitball and threw it at Taryn. I didn't like her anyway. She said I had freckles.

She yelled out, "Miss Ada, Ramoth threw a spitball at me."

Miss Ada came straight back to my desk. "Did you throw that spitball at Taryn?"

"Yes, I did, Miss Ada, but she made a face at me."

"Taryn, did you make a face at Ramoth."

"No, ma'am, I did not."

Wham! Miss Ada popped me on the side of the face, and said, "Ramoth, you behave yourself, you hear me?" I didn't answer.

She turned and went back to the front of the room and continued explaining how the ABC's came about.

It was time now for school to let out, and when the bell rang everyone except me left the room. Miss Ada had not noticed that I was still seated. She had her head buried in the work we had handed in.

4

Finally, when she did look up, she said, "Ramoth, what are you doing here? Didn't you hear that bell ring? The school bus is going to leave you."

I sat perfectly still and stared straight ahead.

"Ramoth," she said, "didn't you hear me? Get up and get on that bus."

I still sat there. "What is wrong with you, Ramoth? Did you hear what I said?"

"Yes, ma'am, I did."

"Then what is your trouble? What do you want?"

"I want my gingerbread man back."

"You're not getting it back. Get up from your desk and get out of here now."

I left the room, ran and jumped on the bus.

When I got home mama asked, "What did Miss Ada say when you gave her the gingerbread man?"

"Oh, she said it was nice of you to do that; but, Mama, I don't think Uncle Hobson should marry Miss Ada; she isn't very nice."

Hesitant

How do I love thee?
Let me count the ways,
I find I'm tongue-tied
And may be for days.

5

Retired

When asked if he was retired, the elderly gentleman replied, "I'm with Ho-Mo-Go."
"I'm not familiar with that organization," the casual acquaintance said. "Who are they?"
"Well, in the Spring I hoe, in the summer I mow, and in the winter I go."

Verity 1

The tentacles of passion
become less gripping
With increased frequency
of irate lipping.

THE ZODIAC

I have found the Zodiac
Just the place for my attack:
First we have Aries up front,
Always there ready to punt.
Taurus, then is next in line
Give me gold or money, gifts are fine.

And Gemini talks with its hands
Fibs and lies--no, just expands.
With Cancer you need to know
They are there to nurture and sew.

And if you need to caress
Leo's there and won't take less.
Now if you think you know how
Just ask Virgo for a bow.

Then look to Libra, she's fair;
Really, no one else does compare.
And if you like a secret
Scorpio will just keep it.

But Sagittarius doth speak
Not always couth, not always meek,
As Capricorn faces life
Just like someone who has strife.

'Cause different Aquarius
Approves of the various,
As Pisces sits and laments
Over the others' comments.

Space at a Premium

Five of the elderly ladies living at the upperclass retirement home were all opera fans. In fact, two of them had been on the opera stage, albeit not internationally.

An outstanding singer, one of world status, was booked to appear at the nearby opera house. And although each of the elderly ladies had physical handicaps, their mental alertness and appreciation for opera had not waned.

On the night of the performance, rather than taking the retirement home's courtesy bus, one of them drove and the other four rode with her. They agreed that in order to get a handicapped parking space it would be wise to arrive at least an hour earlier than usual because of the prominence of the singer.

They left in plenty of time and drove into the parking lot, then over to the Reserved for Handicapped area, up near the main entrance. There was only one space left. As they drove closer another car approached and both came nose-to-nose for the one remaining space.

Both drivers held their ground, staring at each other. Finally, the woman driver in the other car alighted and stood in the space, at which time the driver of the car with the elderly ladies got out, walked over to her. And just as she was beginning to speak, the other woman said, "If you wouldn't mind, my husband has just had surgery, and there is only one space left."

With that, the elderly woman driver said, "My dear, I understand your needs, but we have a total of three hip replacements, five kneecaps and two ruptured discs in our car."

The impasse was over.

The other woman gritted her teeth, said nothing, just hurriedly got in her car with her husband and drove off.

The five retirement home residents parked in the space, and found the evening's performance the highlight of the season.

The Elderly One

She sat across the aisle, all wrapped in age. Her hair was gray and thin besides. You could tell it once was thick and strong, and maybe wavy, too. But now the ailing strands reached out to cover her tiny scalp.

Even her daughter's talented hands had not been able to wash and set it so that she was free from age...old, old age. It did, however, look clean.

Her face was small and wrinkled...oh, so wrinkled. The lines ran east and west, north and south, with intersections in between, some major, some minor.

The hands were filled with a network of veins, and all were prominent.

This little bundle of frailty sat quietly in her seat.

Her tiny blue eyes looked not afar.

And then the flight attendant came upon the scene.

"Good morning, ma'am. Would you like a beverage before lunch?"

"Yes. Give me a double scotch on the rocks."

"All right," the composed attendant reluctantly replied.

We sailed above the clouds; enjoyed our lunch.

And when we reached our destination and were taxiing to the gate, the flight attendant, in her helpful tone, said,

"Ma'am, if you will just keep your seat until the rest have deplaned, I will help you to the exit and they will have a wheelchair for you."

"For me? You must be kidding. Give me another double."

"I'm sorry, ma'am, regulations do not permit us to serve alcoholic beverages once we're on the ground."

"What are you saying? I paid for my ticket, and I will not leave this plane until I get another scotch, you hear, and a double one at that."

I rose to leave and slouched across from my window seat, toward the aisle,

And as I did my eyes met hers. I smiled.

"Young man," she said, "You have done nothing but write ever since you got on this plane."

"I know," I said, "and mostly about you."

"Me?"

"Yes."

"Well," she muttered in a belligerent but assured manner, "you have excellent taste in subject matter."

"We agree."

The flight attendant interrupted: "We have the wheelchair ready now, ma'am, if you will just come with me."

"Is my daughter-in-law out there?"

"I don't know."

"I hope not, the prissy bitch. Her name's Florine.

"She never should have married my son; he's too good for her.

"Oh, goodbye, Captain! Say, you're a good-looking son-of-a-gun."

"Thank you. It was nice to have you onboard. Have a good day."

"Listen to him, will you. Who the hell does he think he is?

"Oh, dear, there's that prissy bitch. Hi, Florine, my darling; I'm so happy to see you."

Useful Donation

Please help me now, both large and small,
The young, the old, yes, one and all.
I know today of some who should,
But have not once since babyhood.
Most people say that I am used,
And there are those who have abused.
Some are generous when they donate,
Often enough to procreate.
But I will not abandon you;
I'm here to stay, and see it through.
I'm for the oldster and the youngster,
Still waiting, yes, your Trusty Dumpster.

The Neighbor's Soup

Always a joker, my alert neighbor spotted me on the front porch and asked if I had tried the soup everyone was raving about. "It's called 'gold soup.'"

"No, I don't think I have. Did you say 'gold,' g-o-l-d?"

"Yes, gold soup, and it's delicious," she said, "and so simple to make. All you need is 14 carrots."

Weddings have their humorous side, and here the participants are matched with our fine-feathered friends, and the activities generally associated with such affairs. (Source: Audubon Society's Field Guide to North American Birds)

WEDDING LEXICON

Bride: Cooing Pigeon
Groom: Whip-poor-will
Maid of Honor: Tufted Titmouse
Best Man: Albatross Sympathizer
Bridesmaids: Beautiful Coots
Groomsmen: Friendly Grouse
Organist: Saw-Whet Owl
Soloist: Yellow-rumped Warbler
Ushers: Prairie Chickens
Ring Bearer: Young Towhee
Preacher: The Red-robed Cardinal
Wedding Gown: White Grosbeak
Bridal Bouquet: Stomach Swallow
The Vows: Great Crested Flycatcher
Invitations: Sapsucker Brochures
Rehearsal Dinner: Spoonbill Payoff
Wedding Reception: Quail Underclass
Honeymoon: The Hummingbird Fright
Thank-You Notes: Raven Appreciation

Resolved in Peace

Court Reporters spend most of their professional life in the courtroom making a verbatim record of trials or taking depositions in law offices. Some also venture into reporting sessions at conventions and board meetings.

A very controversial issue was being discussed, during one meeting I reported. The atmosphere was tense. One member, realizing no progress was being made, asked the chairman for permission to speak.

The request was granted.

"Mr. Chairman," he said, "I am reminded of a statement my grandfather used to make: 'You can lead a horse to drink but you can't make him water.' And I think that's where we are now."

When the twist on the adage permeated the angry minds, the entire board burst into laughter. It relieved the tension, and shortly thereafter the issue was resolved.

Bare Facts

I checked the waste around my waist

In search of all bare facts.

Then saw a need for instant haste

To sign some diet pacts.

15

First Sergeant

Aunt Rosie's militant manner and strident voice over the years had less than endeared her to many family members.

She was absent from the annual reunion when one member suggested building a family-owned retirement home for the elderly relatives, each paying their proportionate share toward its operation. Another suggested that Aunt Rosie be the one in charge, reminding everybody that she was the youngest of the elders, had been a sergeant in military service for her country, and had extensive managerial experience.

"Well," said an uncle, "if you are going to appoint Rosie, 'The Sarge,' to run it, count me out. My Army days are over. No longer will I roll out of bed each morning, stand at attention and salute."

Sarah Phlox

He came to her garden
To pick the flowers
Hoping she would soon liven
His drooping powers.

A Painful Cleansing

Our tiny church was in a small town. It would seat about a hundred people if everybody sat close to one another.

The new preacher had a pretty wife, and neither was more than 30. He was a conscientious messenger from Above, and my relatives said he and his wife were good Christians. Mrs. Veale, however--she was one of the church's staunchest members--told my mother she had seen Pastor Duncan looking at Thelma Lou's legs longer than he needed to. But she qualified the statement with, "I suppose a man is a man, and no woman is going to change a man."

Now Thelma Lou played the piano for Sunday School and then the organ for preaching services.

I liked Thelma Lou because she played hymns in a way they could be enjoyed, and always played them as they were written. But just before the preacher was ready to deliver his sermon, my father and Mr. Frank would pass the collection plate. It was at that time that Thelma Lou played beautiful classical religious selections. Some of the good people said that she had studied under a teacher who had been a student of Ignace Jan Paderewski. Few knew who he was, but mama told me about Mr. Paderewski. Mama played, too, but not like Thelma Lou.

It was the practice each Sunday, once the services were over, for a different family to invite the preacher to join them for the noon meal. And during the week he would always visit some of the parishioners. We were no exception.

It was a Wednesday. I distinctly remember that because Uncle Linwood had a chicken and egg route, and he always stopped by our house on Wednesdays for the noon meal. We called it dinner, but the "fancy" people called it lunch.

17

As soon as Uncle Linwood left the house two of my brothers and I ran to the garage, got the hidden deck of cards and began playing.

We played there not because it was raining or the sun was too hot, but because good people didn't play cards, at least out in the open. And although mama and daddy didn't pressure us about the issue, we knew they preferred that we play checkers. They just closed their eyes to the harmless card games we played in the garage, behind the barn, and in the woods.

We had been playing an hour or more when Pastor and Mrs. Duncan drove up. Daddy had already gone back to the field to plow. I stopped playing and ran out to see them.

"Won't you come in," my mother said as they stepped from the car.

"Thank you," said Pastor Duncan. "Mrs. Reese, how are you and Ramoth?"

"We're fine, thank you."

"We just wanted to stop by and see how things are going and to have a little prayer. Where are the other children?"

"I don't know," said my mother. "They were out in the back yard playing just a few minutes ago."

"No we weren't, Mama," I said. "We've been in the garage playing cards for over an hour."

It was not possible to mistake the look she gave me. The preacher helped allay her embarrassment by saying, "The Lord's youngsters will be youngsters, won't they, Mrs. Reese?"

"You're right," my mother said; and then the preacher told her about their visit with Thelma Lou just before coming to our house.

Anyway, my brothers never came out, and so the four

of us sat on the porch. Pastor Duncan told us about his sick aunt in Raleigh. She had cancer, he said. Mrs. Duncan said her mother was doing quite well after the operation for appendicitis.

They didn't stay long. I wish they had.

As they were readying to leave, Pastor Duncan asked us to bow our heads for a prayer. I remember it well. He prayed to the Lord that He would bless our family, and look after us. And then he thanked Him for the great cooks in the church, mentioning my mother specifically.

He ended his prayer with these words--and to this day I've never forgotten them: "Lord, look down on this fine family, and grant each of them what they so rightly deserve."

Once they drove out of our yard, mama looked over at me and said, "Go to that oak tree over there and break me a switch. And don't get one too small either."

I did as I was told. And as I walked toward her, she said, "The next time the preacher asks me a question, you let me answer."

And then she gave me what I so rightly deserved.

Medical Dictionary

Doctor:	One who practices on you
Medicine:	Expensive purchase; sometimes worth it, sometimes a waste of money
Prescription:	Any substance prescribed by doctors for experimental purposes
Surgeons:	Skilled scalpers
Specialists:	Degreed takers
Anesthetist:	A knocker-outer
Operating Room:	Creative extraction lab serving as the main carving area
Hospital:	House of ill dispute
Nursing Home:	Inactive geriatric gym
Orderly:	Relief personnel
Nurse:	Pill and Pressure specialist
Doctor's Waiting Room:	Pit of pain
Doctor's Examining Room:	Revelation booth
Doctor's Billing Dept.:	Extraction Office
Doctor's Associates:	Accessories to the issue at hand

Divorce Matters

Marriage:	A chronic condition where acute distress is interspersed
Outside Love Interest:	A crutch to help fill the gap
Workaholic:	A spouse who can't stand the mate
Separation:	Temporary relief with long-term effects
Lawyer:	The bridge between husband's and wife's joint assets
Palimony:	Overpayment for an informal agreement
Alimony:	High interest on a bad investment
Support:	Immediate cash for widening differences
Child Custody Order:	The granting of offspring to the better actor
Girlfriend:	A releaser
Boyfriend:	A Wife's releaser
Stipulation:	Attorney's written verbiage on what each shall do but doesn't
Decree:	An order dissolving the mal-contract
Judge:	One who legalizes the culmination of mistakes
Assets:	The tangible and intangible property divided disproportionately among spouses and attorneys
Evidence:	Believable fabrication
Declaration of Intention:	Legal parlance for temporary promises
Minors:	Younger mistakes
Children of Age:	Older mistakes
Exhibits:	Documents attesting to each spouse's major and minor faults

21

Vanity

As I stand before the mirror

Vanity plays its tricks.

I'm forced to see the beauty

In wrinkles, sags and tics.

Liberation

Some people want their art abstract
And others want their sex in bed
But one sure thing that is a fact
It matters not if they are wed.

P. S. to the Epitaph

Throughout her adult life the kindly mother of four had made it known to her family that when she died the one thing she wanted most was a beautiful tombstone. For years before her death there had always been disagreements, arguments and problems among her daughter and three sons, all now long grown. The situation did not improve at the time of their widowed mother's demise.

After the funeral harsh words and disagreements ensued over who would pay to carry out her only wish: a beautiful tombstone. Not one could agree with anyone else. In each case it was further evidence of a cheapness the family had, even toward their own mother. And so they avoided the subject altogether, and the mother's grave remained without a tombstone.

Finally, her only son-in-law--an ex-son-in-law at that--realizing the kind woman would be without her dearest wish, purchased a pink marble tombstone, and asked the engraver to inscribe the usual birth and death information, and then said, "Put this across the bottom:

"P.S.: In memory of a wonderful woman.

"'This headstone was bought and paid for by her son-in-law.'"

Matrimonial Dictionary

Engagement: Premature mental ejaculation

Fiancée: The victorious female

Fiancé: The defeated male

Shower: The bride's extortion of relatives and friends

Wedding: A crash course in Heightened Yearning

Reception: The celebration for an upcoming voyage of reruns

Wedding Gifts: Rewards from relatives and friends to the blissful bride for an upcoming mistake

The Vows: Verbal prescription for health, happiness and another's ways

The Bride: A dove-hawk who coos and captures

The Groom: A man defrocked of all but clothes

Maid of Honor: The prime accessory

Best Man: The prime witness to a grave misfortune

The Honeymoon:	A time-release capsule of euphoric overdosing
Thank-You Notes:	The release of guilt for accepting bribes
Matrimony:	The sacrament for the earthly state of purgatory
Marriage:	A legal bonding of two incompatible elements

Last Meal

At noontime just before the old gentleman was scheduled for discharge from a seven-day hospital stay, the attendant brought in his lunch and, in a cheerful voice, said, "Sir, I am bringing you your last meal."

"Well, thank you," said the old fellow. "What time did they schedule my hanging?"

25

Mrs. O'Leary

Each night at dinner Mrs. O'Leary called on a different boarder to ask the blessing. On Sunday she served a big pot roast, and then served the leftovers on Monday and Tuesday evenings.

When Lloyd was called on Wednesday, he saw yet more evidence of the same.

"Let us bow our heads," he said. "Hebrews 13:8. Amen."

Another boarder turned to his friend and asked, "What did he say?" and the friend responded, "He said, 'Jesus Christ the same yesterday, and today, and forever.'"

The Truth Will Out

"May I ask, Ma'am, why you chose to use a bow and arrow to kill your husband?," inquired the officer.

"Yes, you may," replied the woman. "It was at night you know?"

"Yes, I understand it was."

"Well, it was the quietest way I knew, and I didn't want to wake up the kids."

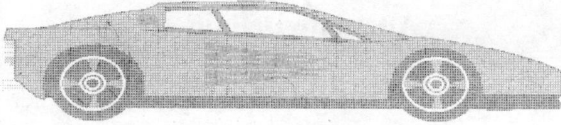

Not in Stock

"I am wondering if you have a certain kind of car in stock?" inquired the middle-aged woman on the phone to the car salesman. "I used to own one years ago, and it was the best car I've ever had. That was some years ago, though."

"Well, ma'am," asked the new light-hearted salesman, "what kind of car was it? Do you remember?"

"That's my problem," she answered. "I don't know. You see, my memory isn't as good as it used to be, and I have a tendency to forget, especially if they are mechanical matters.

"I remember that it was a four-door, and I think it was deep blue, but I am not certain. I know it was a dark color. That much I do know."

"Of course, you realize, ma'am, that won't be of much help. Could you tell us whether it was a Ford, Chevrolet, Buick, or whatever?"

"No, I can't, I'm sorry. All I remember is, it starts with "T."

"After some hesitation, the salesman said, "I'm sorry, ma'am, but we just can't help you. All of our cars start with gas."

Alternate Definitions

Nymphomaniac: The gal who never reaches her goal

Chastity: The state of chronic regret

Pregnancy: A splendid time for growth from within

Asexual: An uneducated condition

Period: The lover's mourning days

Lover's Den: The ploy/joy pit

Sexual aberration: Practices not sanctioned by the inhibited

Erotica: Physical response to mental stimulus, resulting in kaleidoscopical dreams

Precious Jewel: The Gem of Love, admired by many, possessed by few

Latency: Perhaps, unsure, maybe, could be, too late

Promiscuity: Yes.
                                Yes.
                                            Yes.
                                                      Yes.

Yield

My mother was an excellent driver, and except for lightly bumping the front of the garage door when she was learning to drive on her own--while my father was not around--her record was flawless throughout her eighty-five years. However, in her early eighties her judgment and reflexes began to lessen.

I was visiting one weekend and she was driving me out to see a new home being built on the opposite side of the small town. She was not a fast driver, and usually very alert. We were coming up to a "yield" intersection. As we got closer I realized she wasn't letting up on the accelerator, so I said, "Mama, that's a 'yield' sign."

Without a moment's hesitation, she shot right back, "They'll yield," and kept on going.

Does It Really Matter?

While riding on the city bus the elderly lady began a conversation with the middle-aged gentleman sitting next to her. They spoke on several subjects and then the kindly woman asked the gentleman, "Of what persuasion are you?"

"Well, I'm not exactly sure," said the gentleman.

"Oh," said the woman. "What do you mean?"

"It varies; sometimes I go to the Methodist church, sometimes to the Baptist church and sometimes I go to the Presbyterian church."

"Well, what do you call yourself?"

"I call myself a MethoBapTerian."

29

Pastels

Our brain is framed in bone
Better it be pastels
Then we could change its tone

Belly Dancing

While hospitalized for a gallbladder operation in St. Joseph's Hospital in Asheville, I was visited by one of the Staff Sisters, to wish me well and say a prayer.

We spoke about my operation, and I told her it was an 8-inch incision, and then jokingly added that it probably meant the end of my belly dancing days.

For a brief moment she looked shocked, and then said, "Well, you know, they had belly dancers in Jesus' day."

I asked, "Were they accepted?"

"Oh, yes," she said, and then we went on with our regular discussion, and she ended with a beautiful prayer.

The Local Hotel

Without either of the two having any knowledge of Spanish, the young man and his traveling companion headed via air to visit a Latin country they had read about.

Both were of an adventurous nature. Upon landing at the airport they asked, through an interpreter at the curbside, to tell the driver that they wanted to be taken to a hotel that was not one where tourists usually stayed.

"We want to experience the country as the natives live it; we want to savor the real flavor."

The interpreter told them of several moderately priced hotels, but reminded them that they were staffed by only Spanish speaking personnel, and most often frequented by the citizens of the country.

"Fine," said the traveler, "that's exactly what we want. We want to get the real feel of the land."

And with that, their cab arrived. The driver drove them to the designated hotel and, in broken English, told them the amount of the fare.

Once inside, they approached the registration desk and showed their identification. Through facial and hand movement, they managed to get across to the clerk on duty to understand that they wanted to remain for several nights.

They were shown their room. Their baggage was placed inside, and the bellboy was given a tip in U. S. currency.

It had been a tiring overnight trip and the young man decided he wanted to take a shower. He went into the bathroom and found no soap. He stepped out into the hall and spotted a maid.

He had been told that many Spanish words often parallel the English word, and he assumed that the word for "soap" would be one of those. That seemed logical. So he motioned to the maid to come over.

"Buenas dias, Senor y Senora."

"Thank you," said the two travelers.

"Como esta?"

"We don't speak Spanish," said the guy, "but we need some sopa; we want to take a shower."

"Sopa? Yo no comprendo. Sopa?"

"Yes, sopa. We need to take a shower; it's been a long overnight trip."

"Sopa en la mañana?"

"Honey," said the guy, "do you know what she's saying?"

"No, I don't, but why don't you show her what you want?"

"Come," he said, "I'll show you," as he motioned for the maid to come inside the room.

He walked into the bathroom, pulled the shower curtain back, pointed to the empty soap dish and then, with his hands and arms, simulated soaping his upper torso.

"Oh, yo comprendo ahora. No, sopa. Jabon."

"What?" asked the traveler.

"Jabon, jabon."

"Ah," he said. "So the word for 'soap' is 'jabon.' Okay."

He had now mastered Lesson One. In asking for sopa he had been asking for "soup" with which to shower.

"En este momento," said the maid. She disappeared and very quickly returned with two bars of soap.

* * *

"Honey, if it's all right, I'll take the first shower."

"Go ahead," she said.

He pulled the curtain back, stepped in the tub and

looked down at the hot/cold controls. Obviously, he thought, the C stands for "cold" and the F, whatever that is, has to stand for "hot." And so, full force, he turned the C control on and out came steaming water. He had now learned Lesson Two: C stood for the word "caliente," meaning hot. And the F turned out to stand for "frio," meaning "cold."

After they returned from their trip and related their experiences, they both decided to sign up for a course in Spanish at the local college. A bit late, but they knew it was a wise investment for future visits to other Spanish-speaking countries.

Funeral Glossary

Funeral Home:

Initial meeting place for the family's financial disagreements

Casket Spray:

The family's token depreciation

Last Rites:

The final Amendment Rights administered by another

Funeral Music:

A solemn melodious attempt to cover the real problem.

Eulogy:

The opportunity afforded one to redeem him- or herself for the things said about the deceased

Trip from the
funeral home to
cemetery: A one-way trip to the unknown

The bill: Charges made for disposition before
                             family opposition

Family's return
from cemetery: The last togetherness-ride before
                             separateness takes over

Balance is Essential

The youthful newly-weds were dividing the respective household chores.

"And you get to balance the checkbook," she said.

"But, Sweetheart," he shot back, "we don't even have a pair of scales."

Ho-Hum

She's one
In charge of words
She puts them all in rhyme
But brings results of sheer ho-hum
Almost every time.

▼ ▼ ▼ ▼ ▼ ▼ ▼ ▼ ▼

Confusing

The third grade teacher was dedicated, and always tried to have each of her students fully understand her explanations of life, nature and people.

During this one class she was extolling the many wonders of nature and cited as an example, a small chicken getting out of the shell when it is first born.

One of her brighter students had been listening intently, and raised his hand to speak.

"Yes, Reginald."

"What I don't understand about that is how the little chicken gets in in the first place."

Facing Bare Facts

I stepped from the shower

    and stood before the mirror.

A shock of despair

could not have been clearer.

Although nothing was missing

a lot needed repair.

And so it was quite obvious

I didn't have a prayer.

Janice Jean Series
(Cast of Characters)

Daughter:	Janice Jean
Father and Mother	Ruford and Avarena
Uncle (mother's side):	Peter Alex
Uncle Peter's wife:	Thelma Marie
Uncle Peter's daughter:	Tina Sue

Uncle (mother's side):	Clinas Clayton
Aunt (mother's side):	Bertha Biling
Aunt (mother's side):	Pearl Stringer
Janice Jean's brothers:	Billy Bob
	Lonnie Lee
	Alfred Aron
Janice Jean's cousin:	Plethora Mae
Uncle (father's side):	Cyril Clarence

Janice Jean (1)

Janice Jean had three brothers. Two of them were Billy Bob and Lonnie Lee, four years apart.

Billy Bob had a pig, Bossy, he was raising under a 4-H project. One day the two boys were in the back yard eating watermelon from their daddy's patch. Billy Bob insisted that Lonnie Lee give his rind to Bossy. Lonnie Lee refused, and shortly thereafter a running chase ensued. When Lonnie Lee realized he was going to be caught, he stopped, turned around and threw the rind in Billy Bob's face.

It fell to the ground, breaking into many pieces. Their daddy, walking in from his large acreage of watermelons, came upon the scene and inquired of their actions. Each

37

explained his side of the story.

Their father then said, "With all the watermelons we have and you two have to fight over a rind. I'll take care of that."

He then presented his side: a stinging switch to each of their backsides.

Janice Jean (2)

Janice Jean's mother was talented in a number of ways, and my mother and her mother attended the same small church. They often had Circle meetings, I think they called them, in which many church "doings" were discussed.

Now, Janice Jean's mother played the piano by ear, and she also had a reputation for trying to use big words.

One day at the Circle meeting, the president of the group asked for a volunteer to play the piano. Some said they couldn't; others, a bit modest, said they were not really good at it. And everybody knew Janice Jean's mother played by ear, and very beautifully, albeit loud.

"Avarena, how about you?" asked the President.

"All right," said Janice Jean's mother. "I'm not very good at it, but I'll get up there and try to urinate on it."

Of course she didn't, but she did play beautifully.

Janice Jean (3)

Janice Jean's Aunt Pearl was not particularly adroit, but she more than made up for this through her kindness. Age, however, did not treat her too kindly in many aspects, and the older she got the more careless she became.

She was always fond of birds, and had a special place in her heart for humming birds.

Janice Jean and her cousin, Plethora Mae, were visiting one day.

"Have some M & M's," offered Aunt Pearl.

They each took a few from the dish, began to chew, and Plethora Mae said, "Aunt Pearl, what's wrong with these M & M's? They taste funny."

"I don't know," said Aunt Pearl. "I found a crippled humming bird out by the rose bush two days ago, and brought him in and put him in that candy dish. This morning when I looked, he was dead."

"And what did you do with the dead humming bird?" asked her niece.

"Well, I felt sorry for him, so I took him out of the candy dish and put the M & M's in it, and then I put him in a saucer and put it in the refrigerator. Poor thing. Go take a look; he's right there on the top shelf, right beside the tuna fish salad."

Janice Jean (4)

One of Janice Jean's aunts on her mother's side of the family wasn't the best driver around, and from time to time her driving was unpredictable.

She was stopped one afternoon by an officer.

"You realize, don't you, ma'am, that you ran the stop sign back there at the intersection?"

With her head slightly bowed, she meekly answered,

"Yes, I did do that, Officer. I'm sorry."

"May I see your license, please."

She handed her license to him, waited while he was

recording the information. And then, hoping he would be lenient, said, "You probably noticed, Officer, that today is my birthday?"

"Oh, so it is. Well, Happy Birthday!" said the officer, as he handed her the ticket, smiled, and turned to leave.

Janice Jean (5)

Janice Jean's family had only outdoor plumbing and indoor potties. One night one of her brothers, Alfred Aron, came home a bit late, went to bed unnoticed by the rest of the family. He had had one too many beers, and became sick, got up and pulled the "slopjar" from under the bedside and vomited, and then went back to bed.

The next morning Janice Jean's mother said, "Alfred Aron, I thought I heard you stirring last night. What were you doing? It sounded like you were vomiting. What was wrong?"

"Mama, I don't know. After the ball game I ate some cheese crackers, and I guess they were stale."

Janice Jean (6)

Janice Jean had many uncles, and although Cyril Clarence was not her favorite, he was still kind but stern.

Uncle Cyril Clarence, a young widower with four children, had married a widow with three young ones. Later, the two of them had three of their own. They lived in a big old frame house out in the country, where there was plenty of room for the ten kids to roam and play.

As kids will do, they got into a fight one day out in the

front yard, and it was right at the time that Uncle Cyril Clarence was driving in.

Never one to mince words, he jumped from his car, surveyed the situation, rushed to the front doorsteps and yelled to his wife, "Sweetheart,. Sweetheart, come out here quick and help me. Your children and my children are beating the hell out of our children."

Janice Jean (7)

Janice Jean's mother was ugly, and everybody said Janice Jean looked just like her mother. I was taught that "pretty is as pretty does," and so that fact did not disturb me; I liked her for being herself.

Her family was poor. Mine was, too, but we did have a hen house for our chickens to roost in, and Janice Jean's family did not. Each night near dark their chickens would fly up on their porch banister to roost. Now, unlike dogs, chickens cannot be housebroken, so each morning Janice Jean would have to take a bucket of water and the straw broom and clean off the porch floor. But Janice Jean was clever, and it did not take her long to figure out a method to remedy the unpleasant task.

She would wait until the chickens were asleep, and then go down the line and gently lift each one, turn them around so that their derrieres were hanging over the banister on the yard side.

Janice Jean was smart; she no longer had to clean the porch.

Janice Jean (8)

Janice Jean had an aunt who was married to her mother's youngest brother, Peter Alexander. Aunt Thelma Marie bore her uncle his first child, Tina Sue.

Janice Jean, her mother and daddy were visiting the proud new parents. Thelma Marie, not the epitome of upper crust, held the baby in her lap while the family ate, and whenever it began to fret, Thelma Marie would stick a pacifier in the baby's mouth. Sometimes she would spit it out, and Thelma Marie would just pick it up, dunk it in the only sugar bowl on the table, and then put it back in her mouth.

Tina Sue would be contented for a while, until the sweet stuff wore off, and then she would again spit it out, and Aunt Thelma Marie would pick it up, douse it back in the sugar bowl, and put it back in the baby's mouth. The same process occurred over and over again.

It was hot that day, and everybody was thirsty, but it turned out to be a big day for unsweetened tea.

Janice Jean (9)

Janice Jean had an aunt, Bertha Biling, who was a bit uppity, at least in Janice Jean's opinion.

She lived in town, had a beautiful home, and was persnickety about her household effects, particularly her collection of trinkets and knickknacks.

She also owned Pierre, a parrot, and a smart bird he was. He was kept in her "showroom" she called it, just off the dining room. And she taught Pierre many words and phrases.

One day Janice Jean and her mother were visiting.

"Just go on in the 'showroom' and take off your coats

and see my latest collection. They're there on the display shelf on the right."

They went in, took off their coats and were picking up the new additions, examining and admiring them.

Aunt Bertha was still in the kitchen preparing food when she heard Pierre yell, "Bertha, Bertha, they're pilfering in here; Bertha, Bertha, they pilfering in here."

❧

Conservative

"I'm going to have them come out here and cut off the electricity," said the old mountain farmer. "Every time I get a bill they've raised the rate."

"But, Granddaddy," said his teenage granddaughter, "you can't do that. How will you watch television?"

"No problem," he said. "We'll just use a kerosene lamp."

Statistics

While addressing a convention group of three thousand seated delegates, the expert doctor was citing various medical statistics:

"Thousands die each year from emphysema," he said, "and most of these deaths are caused by smoking.

"And do you realize," he continued, "that in this country we eat far too much soft food and too little fiber. We do. You might be surprised to know that reliable data shows that one out of every three adults suffers from hemorrhoids. Think about it, one out of every three. That ought to tell us something.

"So, with that statistic in mind," he added, "if you, yourself, do not suffer from this problem, just look to your immediate left, then to your immediate right--one of them has hemorrhoids."

Evidence at Hand

"There is life after death," moaned the henpecked husband.

"How can you possibly make such a statement?" inquired the wife.

"I'm living proof," he replied.

Marriage Is:

The attempt at bonding two incompatible elements

The probationary period while awaiting divorce

A non-negotiable leash on life

A tainted lifestyle

A way of wife

The Facial Map

I wouldn't mind it so much

If my face showed only interstate lines

But as I grow older

Even the sideroads

Become more obvious.

Medical Specialists

Receptionist - Cover girl

Physical Therapist - Personhandler/ Physical Maneuverer

Gynecologist - Female explorer

Podiatrist - Foot fetisher

Pediatrician - Baby pacifier

Cardiologist - Heart throbber

Neurologist - Nerve connector

Orthopedist - Bone enthusiast

Dermatologist - Skin repairman

Plastic Surgeon - Makeup artist, skin tightener, fill-in man, "substitute" assister, God's dis-owned artists, husband's debtee, wife's savior, miracle perker-upper, face-lifter, boob giver (or taker}, thigh detractor, alter-ego worker, vanity doctor, butcher expert, maskmaker

Dentist - Eater-fixer

Periodontist - Gum savior

Chiropractor - Maladjustment seeker

Orthodontist - Mouth straightener-upper

Pathologist - Disease-man

Psychiatrist - The ill patient's mental doctor

Allergist - Neutralist

Naturopath - Earth-peacer

Rhinologist - A nosy doctor

Rhinolaryngologist - A noisy-nosy doctor

Internist - An inside doctor

Optometrist - A vision man

Opthalmologist - A "sick eye" man

Radiologist - A see-through person

Anesthetist - Personal pain killer

Anesthesiologist - A learned personal pain killer

Inscription

When asked what inscription he would like on his tombstone, the old man said, "Well, my name, date of birth and death; and then just put:

"'This wasn't my idea.'"

The Nursery Policy

"Yesterday I was in here and bought two dozen white petunia plants," said the summer resident to the nursery clerk. "I need six more."

"Right over here" offered the local, whose lower lip, filled with snuff, muffled her words.

"How can you tell they are white?" asked the summer resident. "They are not marked."

"Well, because this is where we keep the white ones and this is where we keep the purple ones, over here."

"But what if I plant them and they turn out not to be white, then what?"

"You just let me know."

"And what will you do?"

"Let'em grow," said the local woman.

Special Request

An 85-year old lady asked her lawyer to handle her funeral arrangements, and was very explicit about the fact that she wanted no men pallbearers, only women pallbearers.

"Women pallbearers?" he asked.

"Yes, only women."

"That's rather unusual, ma'am. May I ask why you want only women pallbearers?"

"Certainly," she answered. "Men don't take me out now so why should I let them take me out then?"

Metamorphosis

Birth: The process by which the warm-blooded mammal comes upon the universal scene in a condition of helplessness, fragility, and innocence.

Living: That state of being between birth and death.

Death: The end result of the combination of birth and living, a result so final that no amount of reconsideration of actions can alter the outcome.

Analysis: We are but one spoke in the Universal wheel, a wheel which turned before our arrival and will turn after we are gone. Our contribution to Eternity is directly proportionate to the efforts expended while on this plane.

It is not too late.

EPITAPH

I think of times one needs to laugh

And those one needs to cry

Then hope my lonely epitaph

Will simply read: "Goodbye."

Yes, You May

"Yes, you may," said my interesting 80-year-old mountain neighbor, "because I'm through feeding Mr. Groundhog. Be my guest."

I was glad to have the use of her garden area. I knew Mr. groundhog could not outsmart me. After all, I was born and raised on a farm in the eastern part of North Carolina, and although we had no groundhogs, we were successful in the battles against other predators. Besides, the almanac says if you plant by certain signs and moon phases you will have more production and fewer pests, and even positive results at weaning children and animals if begun under the correct signs and phases. (Would this apply to the "weaning" of groundhogs from eating vegetables? I would later find out.)

When Spring arrived I had my neighbor's plot plowed, and knew exactly where the beans, corn, lettuce, potatoes, tomatoes and other vegetables would go. The cucumbers, zucchini, yellow squash and pumpkins were in adjoining rows.

I fertilized and limed all areas, omitting, of course, liming the potato rows. They need acid soil. At planting time I bought the best seeds and sturdiest plants. The weather cooperated, and within a few weeks my garden was growing beautifully.

It was a Sunday morning, I remember it clearly. My neighbor had previously asked if I went to church. I explained that I was raised in the Methodist church, and occasionally attended, especially when I visited relatives and friends.

"That's fine," she said. "If you go to church you will be all right." I knew then I had scored a point, but that Sunday morning when I walked over the hill to check the progress in my garden, I am glad the pastor wasn't within hearing distance. There was no doubt the groundhog had visited overnight.

The following day I purchased a "Have-a-Heart" wire cage trap, and within 24 hours captured the offender. Nothing to it; my problem was solved.

Mr. (or Mrs.) Groundhog was taken ten miles away, across the river, and let loose in the beautiful, lush-green Pisgah National Forest. (Any self-respecting groundhog would love to have free room and board in such a government-protected, homey environment.)

So sure was I that the problem was solved, I did not bother to reset the trap, and for days the garden continued to flourish. But then came the second disappointment. It was only then that I knew that my first capture had to have been a "Mrs." because no female could (or would?) do the damage I now faced. The culprit had to be a Mr.

Cut apples were put inside for bait. Another groundhog was caught, slightly larger. It, too, was taken to join, presumably, his mate. Now they could have a second honeymoon, this time in the Pisgah National Forest, at government expense, and do me a favor at the same time.

The trap was reset. A third one was caught. No doubt a sister-in-law. She joined the other two in the new family compound. (The Kennedys aren't the only creatures who have a compound.)

I kept my neighbor informed. "I told you so," she would say.

There was a noticeable letup in the devastation, and I regained new hope. But, never take anything for granted. Wham! One morning I found almost total destruction.

It was at this time that one of the church's teachings came to mind but was quickly drowned by my highly audible tones. Back into operation went the trap. This time not a *fait accompli,* by any means. Days passed as he ate, but not from the trap. So I knew I had at least one more, and well-educated—perhaps holding a Master's in Garden Destruction and a Ph.D. in Outwitting Mankind—still on the loose and plying his trade.

Other neighbors heard my complaints. They suggested I take a rifle and watch the garden in the late mornings, or find the entrance and exit holes and pour mothballs down them, or dynamite the holes, or use a dog to catch them. I was unable the find a hole. So, unwillingly, I shared the struggling garden with the "professor." He was calling the shots.

Autumn arrived, and the pumpkins were beginning to turn orange. I walked through the garden checking, and found a hole under some of the giant wilting zucchini and pumpkin leaves. Ahah! His entrance to nature's paradise. I remembered: They always have an entrance and an exit, so I searched the entire garden, but to no avail. I stepped over the fence and began to search the surrounding area. There, fifteen feet away, in the middle of the briar patch, was the second. Mr. Groundhog had had the perfect setup.

I am sure his home beneath was multi-room, but his prime source of survival was within the garden plot, and all summer I had overlooked the entrance. The "professor" had taken possession by something known in the legal profession as "the law of occupancy." He had lived like the master of his estate and I as the frustrated slave.

It was approaching Fall now, and the season was over. I had lost the battle. But nature's universal truth emerged. I had not starved; neither had the groundhogs. And I had to admit, there was a balance of nature, just as she always intended.

His Honor's Ruling No. 2

Plaintiff's attorney approached the bench and said, "Your Honor, I respectfully request that this case be continued until next week. My wife is due to conceive within the hour."

The Defense attorney stepped forward and said, "Judge, I think my colleague here is a bit nervous this morning. He didn't mean to say that his wife was due to conceive within the hour; he meant to say that his wife was due to deliver within the hour."

The Judge thought for a moment and said, "Well, I am going to grant the continuance because in either instance I think counsel should be there."

The Pros and Cons

Tantrum:
>*Today* - That child needs counseling.
>*Yesterday* - That child needs a good spanking.

Depression:
>*Today* - That child needs a psychiatrist.
>*Yesterday* - That child needs to have grandma talk to
>her.

Problems between the Newly-Married:
>*Today* - They need counseling.
>*Yesterday* - They made their bed; let them lie in it.
>They'll work it out.

Young Drug Addict:
>*Today* - He needs help. Get him in a program.
>*Yesterday* - Keep him busy, show love, and enforce
>discipline.

Peer Presure:
>*Today* - Everybody else does.
>*Yesterday* - When you earn your own money, so can
>you.

Racial Snobbery:
>*Today* - They're wonderful, you know, but...
>*Yesterday* - To each his own.

School Dropouts:
>*Today* - He needs counseling and remedial studies.
>*Yesterday* - He needs discipline and parental love.

Children's Etiquette:
>
> *Today* - Don't correct that child; it may frustrate him.
> *Yesterday* - Sit up, use your fork, not your fingers, or else leave the table.

Business Ethics:
>
> *Today* - Whatever is necessary to make a deal.
> *Yesterday* - One's word and a handshake.

The Student Poet
(Sonnet No. 18)

The teacher taught him rhyme and meter
Impressed them both the same
But never thought for once that Peter
Would be so hard to tame
He sat quite still and asked no questions
Absorbed it all each day
Then quietly followed her suggestions
And did without delay
But once the chores were done in full
He yearned for more aside
'Twas then he was a prancing bull
To show his mounting pride
>
> And though was good his rhyme and meter
> The teacher also liked dear Peter.

Delight

The rooster sits upon his roost
Awaits the hen's invite
He needs no real or helping boost
Because her name's "Delight."

Relative

Whether you call her
        "Ain't," "Ant," or "Ahnt,"
She's still the sister
        of your mother or father;
Unless of course,
        she ain't.
The person then must be
        the brother of your father or mother,
So you call him "Unk," "Unkie" or "Uncle,"
        unless, of course, he ain't.
And if that be a fact,
        call him what you like,
But in either case,
        it's still a relative
Albeit, a bit more quaint.

LaTricia's Lament

She thought that life had been quite fair
Insisted all along
"Twas only how she climbed the stairs
To hear the perfect song.
But when the bells began to ring
And deafened both her ears,
Oh, how she wished that she could sing
To tell of all her years.
But time began to have its way
With stumbling blocks galore,
And never once would she then say,
I've had enough. No more."

COMMA SENSE

We're not inspired by platitudinarians,
Nor those who have untreated biases.
But now we have a host of fresh grammarians
Who give the old a new psoriasis.

Dairy Logic

Love is the cream of life;
Rejection, sour milk.
Deception is mostly skim,
And fickleness, buttermilk.

The High Salute

It was during World War II that our government took over hotels in many areas of the country. They were used by the military personnel to house and train new recruits and inductees.

After induction at an army military installation in Virginia, I, along with many others, boarded a special train and headed north. Upon arriving in Atlantic City we were bused to the famous Traymoor Hotel alongside the Boardwalk.

This luxury piece of architecture had been a mecca for those who could afford the ultimate in hotel accommodations, but a war was on, and unparalleled need for housing for the hundreds of thousands who were called to serve their country.

By the time we arrived, most of the room furnishings had been removed, including the beds, which were replaced with five army cots. Quarters were a bit crowded, but having just been called up, we had not yet amassed many belongings. Bathroom privileges were worked out among us.

Each morning we would eat in the main dining room. After that we lined up and marched onto the Atlantic City Boardwalk. There our sergeant would put us through the paces. At his command, we executed the various drills, improving along the way, and usally marched for long distances up and down the famous Boardwalk. It was during the regular marching that we sang many of the old songs: "...someone's in the kitchen with Dinah, strumming on the old banjo," and "Roll Me Over in the Clover," plus others, some a bit more raunchy than others.

Now, you would have thought that inclement weather would have caused us not to march and practice the drills. Not so. When the weather was bad, in small groups we took turns lining up in the huge lobby of the hotel and continued our drilling, although an abbreviated version.

Kate Smith, the American singer of popular music at that time, rose to prominence on both radio and television. It was she who truly immortalized Irving Berlin's great song, "God Bless America." She belted it out at a sister hotel, and many of us were privileged to have seen and heard her. The song has remained a favorite of millions down through the years, a testimony to her great voice and talent, and the song is still played at both military and civilian functions throughout our country.

Glenn Miller, a great American trombonist and band leader of that day, played for us. He did his part for the soldiers and his country. At the outbreak of World War II he assembled a large band and flew to England, where he played for the Air Force. On December 16, 1944, he was on a flight from England to France when the plane disappeared and has never been heard from since.

Perhaps one of my most memorable occurrences happened during one of the inspections at the Traymoor. All servicemen of that day: Army, Air Force, Navy or Marines, will remember the inspections. They checked the shoes, the uniform and the belt—and each had to be just right, the belts and shoes shining and the uniform neat. Our hair had to be trim. When it came to inspection, there were no excuses.

One inspection in particular that each of us will always remember was a periodic one which was commonly referred to among soliders as the "shortarm" inspection. No World War II Army soldier living today needs an explanation. But for some of their descendants who may be desirous of one, it was an inspection where the military medical officer, and usually an enlisted soldier of a sergeant's rating, would come by as you stood at the foot of your bed. You could be partially clothed, but they would ask you to "strip down"—for lack of a more

59

obscure wording—your male organ. If any type leakage oozed during this pressure stripping, you would then report to the dispensary to be further checked for veneral diseases. If there was no fluid emission on stripping, and the general area appeared normal, you passed, and could carry out your daily duties with a clear mind.

There was, however, at that inspection one embarrassing moment for one of my buddies. Because there was only one bathroom for the five of us, we naturally had to take turns answering nature's calls. On this occasion when the enlisted sergeant entered and yelled, "Attention!" we rose and stood until the lieutenant approached each of us. At this particular "Attention!" one of my buddies happened to be seated on the john, administering to the essential needs indigenous to all Homo sapiens. When he heard "Attention!" yelled as the sergeant entered, he instinctively stood with his underwear and pants at his feet. There, standing rigid, he held his stance as the medical officer approached and stood squarely in front of him.

"At ease," said the lieutenant, and they proceeded to go through with the inspection. My buddie had no leakage. It was at that time the lieutenant said, "Should such an occasion arise again, soldier, this is certainly a situation where you do not have to rise and come to attention."

"Thank you, sir," said my buddy, still facing straight ahead.

The medical personnel left the room and my buddy finished the natural project, dressed and joined the rest of us as we proceeded to go downstairs for the lineup prior to another march on the Boardwalk. We laughed about "John-boy's" extraordinary experience until basic training was over and were deployed to various other military bases to fulfill the obligations our country had to meet at that time.

Commands

"You may go;
"You wait.
"Now you may go,
"And you wait."
Here I stand
Giving commands.
Seldom does one
Disobey my orders.
I often think
Without me the world
Would be delayed.
But then my job
Is a simple one:
First I'm green
And then I'm red.
You see, I'm a stoplight.

The Cow's Tall Tale

A friend was telling me of a case he had heard in court about the farmer who made a claim for a train having killed his cow.

"Now, sir, we just want to know the facts here," said counsel. "Was your cow on the tracks?"

"No, sir, she was not. She was a quarter of a mile away. And when the train saw her, it jumped the tracks, ran toward her in the field, and it scared her and she ran up a tree, got hung and strangled to death."

Cliffhanging

I sometimes feel I was born with age
And not because of wrinkles or special brains.
It's just that yesterday has gone
And left me filled with geriatric pains.
So here I am with only now
And hope I hold onto it,
Or else I'll have to figure out
A way I can renew it.

Estranged

I almost hate to be with you.
When I visit you are so quiet.
I offer you much, but get so
    little in return.
You seem completely passive.
I give you my undivided attention.
I stay close to you.
I never forget for a moment,
    you are so near
And yet I sometimes shiver,
    you are so cold.
John seat, why do you treat me so?

"Christine"

I know she is a work of art,
Abstract though she may be;
But one with which I dare not part,
A priceless piece, you see.

A Choice

The husband wept and tried to find
Just what it was his wife preferred.
He learned to be so very kind
As she was "him'd," and then was "her'd."

At last he thought he was on cue
Until he heard her say with pride
Of all the hims and hers she knew
Not one would she then cast aside.

And so he stood and had his say:
"You must decide between the two:
It's you and me and all the way,
Or else you go and live with Sue."

The Bible is Vulnerable

Few, if any, children grow up without choosing their favorites among family members, including, of course, their parents, siblings, uncles, aunts and grandparents.

And often just as they have favorites, there are some that are not. This doesn't mean that the less-favored remain that way forever. The feeling can last for a few hours, overnight, and even longer. It usually depends on the age of the child and the degree to which he or she perceives the "offense" that brought on the disfavor in the first place.

One of little Johnny's uncles and his wife routinely visited the grandparents every other Sunday. On the Sunday afternoons that they were not visiting his grandparents, they would visit the uncle's sister, little Johnny's mother. On a Sunday that they were to visit Johnny's mother they visited, instead, the grandparents—the second Sunday in a row. This upset Johnny, for he loved being around that particular uncle and aunt. He liked their sense of humor.

On the second Sunday's absence from Johnny's house, he sat down and wrote them a note, but whether it was ever mailed is not known. When the visitation ritual occurred again in the same manner a few weeks later he became more upset, and so he opened the family Bible to that portion that has the blank pages titled "Deaths," "Marriages" and "Births."

Under the pages for "Deaths" he wrote both his uncle's and aunt's names.

Later, he became annoyed at one of his cousins, and although she was not wed, he wrote her name in on the "Marriage" page. And opposite her name he wrote that of the town drunk.

When another of his uncles—at the time a bachelor—didn't visit as often as he thought he should, he thought he would wipe him out by also including his name on the "Death" page.

And then, when he didn't like some of the relatives, he wrote in only a part of each of their names (first or middle), thus giving them a totally different identification.

He had two of his really obnoxious cousins marrying one another, even though they were sister and brother.

It wasn't until Johnny's own sister was cleaning the "company" room and rearranging everything that she was just fanning through the Bible and suddenly saw the pencil writing. She confronted Johnny, who denied all accusations—and in those days the accused was not afforded an attorney, advised of his or her constitutional rights in such situations, nor even given a chance to explain—so his actions were immediately reported to his mother.

"Johnny, did you do that?"

"Mama," his sister interrupted, "it's his handwriting; you can tell that."

"Did you do it, Johnny?" his mother asked again.

"Mama, George Washington cut down the cherry tree, and he said he could not tell a lie."

"I'm asking you, Johnny, not George Washington. Did you write that in the Bible?"

"Yes."

Johnny's sister was then dispatched to bring the hair brush to their mother, who quickly applied the back side of the brush to Johnny's back side.

And since that time, although Johnny may have from time to time had some passing feelings of disenchantment with various family members, he has never again written in the Bible.

Facts

Raisins are grapes
Put out to pasture,
Or maybe on
Social Security.
And Prunes are merely
Plums that need cosmetic
surgery.

The Undertaker

As the local undertaker sat waiting for his car to be repaired in the service station, he was chatting with several other men, all having a good time exchanging jokes.

One of the oldtimers spoke up and said to the undertaker, "You know something, you're the only person I know in town who shakes more hands than a politician."

And then he added, "Tell me, how can you stand there at the entrance to the funeral home dressed in a $500 suit and a $150 pair of shoes and try to put on a sympathetic face?"

Chocolate Mousse

I can't believe the souls around
Who eat the stuff with such gusto,
And never cease to then expound
About the taste and light fluffo.

It is to me a weak fru-fru
Comprised of air and frilly top
That twists the mouth in shape "oo-oo,"
And makes you want to say, "Oh, stop."

Broken Habit

I use to shampoo my hair
And comb it every day.
Time aborted that routine,
Affording me no say.

Attention!

The mind is made of many a part,
And with old age some soon depart.
But doctors now can do repair,
Saving us each from sheer despair.

Just a Second

Vera, new to the rural area, spoke on the phone to the host for the country call-in radio program.

"Sir, I'm a city girl and my husband is also from the city. Neither of us know anything about raising chickens, but last Saturday we purchased six hens and a rooster at the local flea market."

"Yes," commented the host. "And what is your question?"

"Well," she said, "I have noticed that at times the rooster chases the hens around the yard and then he will get on top of one. Is this normal?"

"Absolutely," responded the radio host. "That's how the egg is fertilized."

"But how long is he supposed to stay on top of her?" she inquired.

The host was stumped for a quick answer, and seeking help, he looked at his producer in the control room, and through the earphones he heard him say, "Tell her 'Just a second,' and we'll come up with an answer."

So the host turned to the mike and said, "just a second, ma'am."

At which point the lady said, "Oh, all right, thank you very much; I didn't know."

Shakespeare

I could hardly resist staring as I stepped aboard the scenic bus and took a seat across the aisle from a beautiful young lady sitting beside the older gent. I used every excuse to look in her direction: the sights beyond her window, other passengers nearby, etc.

Finally, the elderly gentleman, looking a bit stern, inquired, "Young man, are you all right?"

"Yes," I replied. "Why do you ask?"

"Because," he said, "me thinks 'yon Cassius has a lean and hungry look.'"

The Aerial Way

**Airplanes aren't on time
But babies crying
And hyena laughs
Are a guarantee
If one flies with regularity.**

The Scarecrow

Back in 1937, while high school freshmen, Robert, Ralph and I were always happy to see a new girl join our class. We lived in the country and our parents were farmers. When Laura Mae's family moved into the area her parents also became farmers, although some said they came from "up North." And to us, "up North" was from a big city, and city people didn't know how to farm.

Neither Robert, Ralph nor I knew her parents, but Laura Mae had what we called that "city" look. In those days girls who possessed it were both a mystery and a pleasure to be around. They were different: Their speech patterns had inflections foreign to ours; they finished their sentences much quicker than we did, and their movements were different. Laura Mae fit that mold, and we stood in awe of this combination.

Although her parents were said to be "kind people from up north," we just couldn't understand why such city types would want to move south to farm. But we were ecstatic that Laura Mae came into our class. It was right after Christmas that they moved down.

As to dating, a car was out of the question for any of the three of us. We were too young to date—at least in our parents' opinions—and we had to "make do" with the time and places we had available at school.

Robert, tall and skinny, with short brown curly hair, struck her fancy. During break periods and recesses they were often standing in the hall talking to one another.

Ralph, although a bit shy, occasionally managed to garner some of her free time, because he was the class brain, and sometimes helped her with math. Additionally, he had that Southern modulated voice that sounds acceptably macho.

Now Laura Mae was not "stuck-up," as we used to say, even though she was truly a beautiful girl, with long, blonde, naturally wavy hair and pale green eyes—a rarity in our area. She had begun to show pleasing upper signs of coming into womanhood, had a tiny waistline, and her hips spoke a language of their own.

She tried to treat all her classmates the same, and only when some of us went a bit overboard in wanting to get too close, would she show signs of dignity that one usually sees in ladies older than Laura Mae.

There was no doubt about it, I had a crush on Laura Mae. Perhaps my feelings were a bit more emotional than either Robert's or Ralph's.

And because our parents were farmers, like most others in the area, we planted a garden each year, protected from birds and other pests by a scarecrow. There was sort of an unacknowledged contest where each family tried to make theirs the most original and life-like.

I had an advantage over Robert and Ralph, though, because Laura Mae and I rode the same school bus. It usually ran the route, backtracking each day at one certain point. Prior to Laura Mae's moving into the community, I had always gotten off the bus as it first passed my house, but I decided to begin riding it around the loop and to get off as it backtracked. This way I was able to talk to her more, and get to know her better without having to share her with Robert and Ralph.

The first afternoon I rode the loop, we sat beside each other. As we rounded the curve to her parents' house, there was her father's garden near the road. Placed upright in the middle of the rows was a pitiful looking figure dressed in an old torn straw-hat, ragged overalls, and a faded checkered shirt. Even a hoe was stuck under the right arm, adding

71

authenticity.

In an effort to gain further favor, I said, "Laura Mae, tell your father he never has to worry about crows eating his garden; any scarecrow that ugly will keep everything away."

At that moment the "scarecrow" began hoeing.

Laura Mae is married now, but not to me.

Education

The teacher was questioning her new students.

"Johnny, what is a cannibal?"

"I'm sorry, ma'am, but I don't know."

"Well, let me ask you this: if you ate your mother and father and sister, what would you be?"

"An orphan."

Time To Repair

The preacher was extolling the benefits of a house cleaning of the soul: "While you are still on the top side of the sod," he said, "remove those boards of stubbornness, and tear down the walls of indifference."

One parishioner asked, "But, Reverend, what if we think we already have a solid foundation?"

"Reinforce, my good man, reinforce," advised the preacher; "otherwise, His wrath may weaken the underpinning."

The Food

The food
You eat aboard
The plane enroute to there
Will make you wish you had remained
Elsewhere.

Any Metal in Your Mouth or Hips

"Rotator cuff tear with adhesive capsulitis," said Doctor Orf, "and I would like for you to have an MRI done over at Angels of Mercy."

My shoulder had made a tearing noise when I slipped on the icy hillside, and it hurt, but I didn't realize I had done that much damage.

"What is an MRI, Doctor?"

"It stands for Magnetic Resonance Imaging. That will pinpoint the location."

His diagnosis was confirmed, and one week later I arrived at the check-in desk of Angels of Mercy.

"Mr. Hart, please answer the questions on this form, and then sign at the X marks: here, here and here."

The form was long, the questions detailed.

"Thank you. Mr. Hart, do you have any metal in your mouth, hips or other portions of your body? Ever had TB? Heart trouble? Lung problems? Do you smoke? High blood pressure? Diabetes?"

I answered in the negative to each.

"Now, if you will, come with me. I'll take you over to our lab and the nurse will do a workup."

"Thank you," I said, and followed.

"Mr. Hart," said the nurse, "first a few questions: Have you any metal in your mouth, hips or other portions of your body? Ever had TB? Heart trouble? Lung problems? Do you smoke? High blood pressure? Diabetes?"

The answers were the same.

"Now we will do an EKG. It looks great to me, but the doctor will have to do the interpreting.

"And now I need a little blood. Just three small vials. Okay. That's fine. It didn't hurt, did it?"

There was no time to answer before the next procedure.

"Also, we will need a urine specimen."

"Miss, I don't know that I can. I didn't realize I would be asked to give, and I just went before checking in."

"Well, we have to have one. Take this bottle into the room over there and see if you can't squeeze out just a wee bit. I don't need much."

Earnest effort begot earnest results, though small. But she had said a small quantity would be sufficient.

"Thank you. And Mr. Hart, before any procedure of this type is performed, we want the patient to speak to Doctor Pauze. He is the gentleman who will explain the anesthesia procedure and tell you exactly what Doctor Orf will do when he manipulates your shoulder."

"Thank you," I said, as I moved to his office.

"Mr. Hart," he began, "you will be put to sleep."

"What do they use for that?"

"Sometimes it is sodium pentothal, sometimes nitrous oxide, but whatever it is, you will be 'under and out,' and you won't feel any pain as he is doing the manipulating. Doctor Orf will do this. You will then be moved to the recovery room, and when you come out from under the anesthesia the nurses will be there with you."

"You say, Doctor, that I will be 'under and out?'"

"Correct. Trust me. Now, if you'll wait outside here, we need to make a few X-rays."

"Mr. Hart, I am the X-ray technician, and my name is Lloyd Reyes. Do you have any metal in your mouth, hips or any other portions of your body? Ever had TB? Heart trouble? Lung problems? Do you smoke? High blood pressure? Diabetes?"

My blood pressure was rising, having to answer the same questions over and over.

"No."

"Stand here, if you will, and pull your shoulders up close. Fine. Now, stand sideways with your left shoulder against the plate. Great. Okay. Just have a seat in the room there and Nurse Alemon will soon come and take you to the Prep Room."

The walk down the hall was short.

"Mr. Hart, do you have any metal in your mouth, hips, or any other portions of your body? Ever had TB? Heart trouble? Lung problems? Do you smoke? High blood pressure? Diabetes?"

The answer was the same.

"All right. Now let's go over to the Operating Room."

"Mr. Hart, I'm Don Overshotte, the anesthetist. We are going to put you to sleep and Doctor Orf will do the manipulation."

I felt myself sinking.

* * *

"Has the doctor arrived yet?"

"Mr. Hart, Dr. Orf has done the manipulation," said

the nurse. "You are now in Recovery, and doing just fine. Just take a deep breath."

I did. "Why do you ask me to do that?"

"Well, sometimes when you are coming out from under, you don't breathe as deeply or as often as you should."

"Okay." I continued to breathe heavily, on and off, and then felt as if I were going to vomit, but a quick shot in the arm quelled the approaching moment.

"Mr. Hart, we are going to move you to our regular In-Patient area. Room 607. You are doing fine. The nurse on duty there will take over."

The roll over was distant.

"How do you feel, Mr. Hart?"

"Not bad, a bit weak and nauseated."

"Drink this water."

"I see I am hooked up to something here."

"Yes, that's the intravenous injection apparatus."

"What's in the clear plastic bag?"

"Well, it is a solution of 5 percent dextrose and 0.45 percent sodium chloride. We are also giving you pain medication at the same time, but you need the two together in order for the medicine to work effectively."

"Fine."

"Now I have to ask you a few questions: Do you have any metal in your mouth, hips or any other portions of your body? Ever had TB? Heart trouble? Lung problems? Do you smoke? High blood pressure? Diabetes?"

Again, I gave the usual answer.

"Here is a urine bottle, if you need it, and you will. We want you to drink fluids and we want you to urinate. We have to get the anesthetic out of your system, and that helps."

"All right."

The large plastic bottle was angled near the top

portion. Did they expect the relief mission to be accomplished while lying flat on the back? No way. Fortunately, there was enough loose tubing to enable me to stand at the bedside. What I didn't realize was that when you remove your body from the bed, it activates a signal at the nurses' station.

"Yes, can I help you?" the brassy voice blurted over the speaker.

"No, thank you; I am just urinating."

"Fine. Please continue."

Shortly after, Nurse Rebel arrived to switch off the mechanism that had been activated when I moved off the bed. As he did so he said, "This way you know and we know that we have been attentive."

"Sir, it is dinnertime and I'm hungry. Will I get any food this evening?"

"Oh, yes. It will be coming up shortly."

Very soon thereafter a lady brought a tray with a small steak--apparently parboiled, oven-dried and grill-glazed, which resembled porcelain. It was resting beside an orphaned potato suffering from atrophy. Placed nearby was a small slice of cake topped with canned cherry filling and a miniature dollop of substitute whipped cream. Not exactly what you'd call gourmet dining.

Despite TV, the night was restless, but the morning was much better; they delivered a newspaper.

"Shortly, Mr. Hart, we will take you down to Physical Therapy. The nurse will instruct you on how to exercise the shoulder and arm. After that you will get a prescription from Doctor Orf, and he will set up an appointment for you to report back to him."

"Thank you." I went to Physical Therapy in a wheel chair.

"Mr. Hart, I'm Rosie, your therapist, and there are

several exercises we want you to do at least three times a day. First, stand facing me and relax. Now move the arm forward and backward, slowly, and don't extend it too far if it begins to hurt; just back off a little. Next, do the same thing with a cross movement like this, you know, in front of you. Now raise your arm all the way up. Okay. Now lie here and hold this stick in your hands, move it up, over and behind your head as far as you can go without pain. Fine. Now do these exercises at least three times a day."

"I can do them more often if that would be better."

"Great. We'd prefer every two hours during the day."

"I will do them every two hours."

"Good. You can go back to your room, get your things, go down stairs and check out."

"Thank you."

The ground floor hadn't changed, nor had the person at the desk.

"Mr. Hart, if you remember, yesterday when you signed in you turned in your watch, billfold and change. I will return them to you, and when I do please check to see that everything is there.

"But first, just a few questions. I know you may have answered them before, but to be sure we have them on record: Have you any metal in your mouth, hips or in any portions of your body? Ever had TB? Heart trouble? Lung problems? Do you smoke? High blood pressure? Diabetes?"

"The answer to all, ma'am, is still no; and, yes, I have answered them once or twice."

"Oh, great. Now here are your personals."

"That's right, $18.25, my watch and billfold. Thanks."

"Mr. Hart, we thank you. Have a nice day, and do come back to see us again sometime soon."

Gelatinous

Love is a many-splendored thing.
Unless it is misspelled.
Then it becomes a many-splintered thing
A sign it never really jelled.

Is It?

I don't know if life is
What it's cracked up to be.
I do know it's the only one
I presently see.

Out of the Mouths

Invited to visit a former classmate who had become successful, married late, and had two young children, I arrived at their impressive Southern colonial home.

While having dinner in the formal dining room, their son, six, said, "Mr. Reese, I'm happy you came today."

"Thank you, " I said. "I'm happy to see your father after all these years and to meet you, your mother and sister. But tell me," I asked, "why are you happy I'm here?"

"Because," he said, "we don't get to eat in this room very often."

Dichotomous

If we call the unmarried male a bachelor,
And the unmarried woman a spinster,
Does that mean he can't use a spatula
Or she never stood before the "min'ster"?
And if we say he is the Master,
Then is she rightly called the Mistress?
Maybe not, for then he'd be the Sir,
And, God forbid, she'd be the Madam.
Perhaps it's better he be the Major.
But then she'd have to be the Majorette?
And let's not forget, if he were Governor,
Of course, we'd say she was Governess?
Have we not gone a bit too far,
Unless, of course, you are a poet
Whose liberties are quite bizarre,
And by now you'll surely know it.

The Village Messenger

The young preacher had been in town only a few weeks. As was the custom, after delivering his Sunday morning sermon, he would stand at the door and shake hands with the members as they left.

One old gent shook his hand and said, "Preacher, that was a horrible sermon you delivered this morning; there wasn't a thing uplifting about it. In fact, to level with you, every one of your sermons have left a lot to be desired. They have not been a bit inspirational."

The young preacher was taken aback, but thanked him for his frankness.

The following Tuesday night when the Board of Trustees met for their regular business meeting, the preacher was in attendance. He told them what the old fellow had said, and then added. "I am a bit concerned, and wonder if that is the feeling of just this one member, or if some of the other members feel the same way."

"Oh, don't pay any attention to him," said one of the board members. "He's the village idiot. All he does is go around repeating what he hears everybody else saying."

Lacking

No one knows the trouble I've seen,
Nor do they really care.
It's not that I'm fat or lean,
It's less and less of hair.

The Fowl Injustice

What shall we name this building?" my father asked.

"Very simple," my mother replied, "just call it 'The Hen House.'"

That was more than half a century ago and fowl injustices involving minorities, namely male chickens, or "roosters," were prevalent. These cocky creatures had little control over the living quarters they shared with hens.

My father was not a male chauvinist, nor my mother a militant feminist. They were busy, however, parenting seven kids, and that could have had something to do with the injustice thrust upon these male creatures of the fowl species, an injustice that has affected and done undeniable harm to every generation of roosters since.

Those many years ago my father built the sturdy 10 x 12 frame house for both sexes. Although rustic, the style offered a charming cathedral-type ceiling.

There was a door in the front large enough for humans to enter, plus a small rectangular vertical opening about five feet from the ground. This was so the chickens could enter and exit at will. He built a wooden ladder-type structure that ran at an angle from the ground to that opening which had a small slatted sliding cover that could be pulled over the opening. This was to prevent 'possums and other nocturnal predators from entering at night.

My father didn't realize the consequences of his actions. He liked the name and was proud of the lettering he skillfully carved on the planking for the sign, which he hung above the door: "The Hen House."

And from that day forward, it was known as "The Hen House."

Although the roosters would have been justified, they

made no fuss over the obvious feminine gender sign hanging on the front where all passersby could readily see it. It was their silence at the outset that has created the problem which exists today. There may be a time to remain silent, but there is also a time to speak out.

As before, generation after generation of chickens have served Homo sapiens in various ways, and yet not once have the roosters organized, formed an alliance, or made a move geared toward financial retribution for this past gross injustice. Unthinkingly, by their inaction, they thrust upon all roosters that have been born since that time the burden of ignominy.

Would it not have been fairer had my mother chosen a name more representative of both sexes? Certainly there were many available.

There is no possible way to estimate the number of rooster generations that have been emotionally scarred, even to the point of not being able to strut and hold erect their combed heads.

Through the years, all roosters have suffered from low self-esteem, had little to crow about. No doubt millions have needed--and probably didn't get--therapy, as will many more in generations to come.

It is time, I believe, for restitution. This thoughtless act warrants a background investigation of my parents, even though they are deceased. Once that is accomplished, there must be consultation with professionals to determine the full extent of the damage done to the male fowl psyche, as well as the impact it has had on subsequent generations. And an all-out effort must be expended to determine the cumulative detrimental effect on those living today. There should be a Presidential apology. This will cost the taxpayers large sums of money, but the results will serve to right an injustice.

And if we are going to be earnest in our efforts, then we must see that our senators and congressmen introduce companion bills that would lead to ultimate compensation for all the male fowl alive today.

This would require the appointment of special committees to set up hearings, so that a combined bill could come before both the House and the Senate for debate and eventual vote.

Members from both sides will no doubt attempt to tack on amendments that provide compensation for future generations of roosters, both "caponic" and "non-caponic." That is to be expected.

Stand up and say it: "No effort is too great nor expense too enormous when it comes to dispensing justice."

Yes, hearings will involve grave fowl references to the issue by both houses. There will be expert testimony by representatives from both genders. But once that is over and the vote has been taken, it most assuredly will be placed on the President's desk for signature. And although he has broad veto power, it is doubtful he would deny these living descendants--and future ones--their rightful inheritance.

Statistically, of course, it is impossible for any of those who were housed in "The Hen House" in those days to be alive today, but their descendants have rights. We are a country of rights. The roosters of that day most assuredly suffered humiliation in silence, living in a place referred to as "The Hen House." A blatant misnomer if ever there was one.

Isn't it logical to assume that my parents, unaware of their wrongdoing, would have wanted to see this injustice righted? You know it is true.

* * *

Just a moment. Someone's at the door.

"Sir, we are from TAFE, 'Treat All Fowl Equaly.'
Would you contribute to a worthy cause? Our primary
purpose today is to rectify the past injustices thrust upon a
minority of yesterday.

"You see, we want to pay retribution to those who
were treated so unfairly in the past, and who, down through
the generations, have grown progressively more neurotic, and
been less attentive to their female counterpart.

"Here's a mini sketch of what we propose. And
despite their crowing, they were a pitiful group, a minority
who had no say--now or ever--when it came to shelter.

"We want to erect this obelisk--this monument, if you
will--for those unfortunates who served all the people of their
day, each in his own way. We want this monument to speak
for those who have heretofore gone totally unrepresented.

"It will list fowl information, cite astounding facts and
figures heretofore undisclosed. It will list the names of the
martyrs. Among those names will be all the roosters who have
suffered down through the generations because of the
inconsiderate act of two unthinking humans.

"It will also be a reminder to those of the species
living, as well as to future generations to come, that every
creature on earth has a right to equality, regardless of gender
or sex orientation.

"Will you contribute? Any donation would be
appreciated, and we will accept your check, credit or debit
card. God bless you."

I gave. I am truly sorry that my parents were so
thoughtless many fowl generations ago, but I couldn't help
that; I was a small child. It is quite obvious, however, that had
my mother suggested calling it "The Fowl House," we
wouldn't have this problem today.

Numbers Help

Farmer Brown stepped up to the ticket booth at the county fair and said to the lady, "Ma'am, my twelve kids here have been pestering me all week; they want to see that prize bull that won the blue ribbon. So, let me have twelve children's tickets and one adult's, if you will."

The manager overheard the conversation, looked over at the father and twelve kids and asked, "Sir, are all these your children?"

"Yes, sir, they sure are, everyone of them."

"Then you may go in for free. I want the prize bull to see you."

Leather Britches

Down South, way down south, they don't always plant the same way or the same vegetables and other crops that they do in the North Carolina mountains. For example, many plants that will grow in Florida won't grow in Carolina's western mountains.

And, likewise, the people can be different, especially some of the oldtimers. Many grew up in rural areas that had no electricity, no modern conveniences, and so they had to make-do by improvising, particularly when it came to preserving the vegetables and fruits raised on the farm. Many still hold to some of these earlier methods of preserving.

A grandson, only ten at the time, born and raised in Florida, came to visit his grandparents, who lived in the beautiful mountains. It was the first time he had visited in their home since he was in diapers. His grandparents picked him up at the airport, brought him to the country place and began to show him around. He was full of questions. They explained everything, told him of their way of living and how they enjoyed living in the mountains, how close it was to nature.

At bedtime, the grandmother said, "Randall, you'll enjoy your visit here, I'm sure. Things are much quieter and we just don't live the fast pace that people do in the big city, like Miami."

"It's sure different, Grandma," said the boy.

"Tomorrow," grandma offered, "we'll have some good old homemade sausage and yard eggs for breakfast, and I'll make you some fresh, hot clabber biscuits. And then for dinner--we eat our dinner in the middle of the day--we'll have some good fried chicken, potatoes and some leather britches."

"Some what?"

"Leather britches? Didn't your mama ever tell you about leather britches?"

"No. The only britches I know about are the kind you wear, but we call them pants and jeans. Did you say they were leather?"

"Yes, leather, leather britches."

"And you eat them?"

"That's right. You see, what you do, you take green beans when they are ready to pick, string them up with a needle and coarse thread and-- Wait a minute, I'll show you."

Grandma went to the pantry and returned with four three-foot long strings of dried cornfield beans. "Now last summer your grandpa and I picked these beans, and then we took a large needle and thread and strung them, just like you see here. And then we hung them up to dry."

"I've never seen anything like that before."

"Well, wait and see; you'll love them. They'll be good,

I can tell you. Before I go to bed I'll pour boiling water over them and let them soak all night. Then tomorrow morning I'll put a ham hock in the pot and cook them 'til they're nice and tender."

"Well, Grandma, why do you call them leather britches?"

"You know something, I thought you'd asked that. Here's the reason: When they are dried outside like that they get tough, tough as leather, and you have to soak them first and then cook them. Otherwise, they take too long to cook, if you just put them in the pot like you see them right here now. You see, they're almost as tough as leather, just like the leather britches I saw you unpack this afternoon, so you can roam these hills tomorrow."

"Yeah, my leather pants. I did bring a pair, and I love to wear them."

"And you wait and see. You can't wear them of course, but I'll guarantee you, you'll love these leather britches."

"One Sugar, Please."

A friend was sailing on a British liner. While lounging on the deck late one breezy morning, a waiter worked his way among the guests offering a hot beverage. When he reached her, he bowed slightly, smiled and offered her a cup.

She nodded and said, "Yes, if you please, and one sugar."

"Sugar, madam? In your broth?"

Hope

"You say you love me for what I'm not and hate me for what I am," said the weary wife. "I don't know where I stand."

"Then sit," the elderly husband said. "Now, is there anything in between?"

Arguments for the Proper
Salutation and Other Usages

Just as many of the words in our language have the prefix or suffix "man," and bearing in mind all the hoopla it has caused in recent years, such as: the push by some to change manpower to personpower, and manhole cover to personhole cover, etc., should not some thought be given to altering some of our words that begin with "hell"?

After all, none of us can dispute the fact that the word "hell," standing alone, has a negative connotation. And certainly we have enough negativity without piling on more.

How about changing hell-raiser to heaven-raiser. It might just change the ways of many. Certainly no one can object to someone working toward a lofty goal or for a godly cause.

And hellhound--the dog represented in mythology as a guardian of the underworld--if we changed that to heavenhound, we might do away with the underworld and at the same time have all the canine society on our side.

Don't forget "Hello!" We use that to greet another, and usually with positive thought. But when you analyze it, dissect it, and pronounce the two syllables, "Hell-o," don't you hear the "Hell"? And you don't really mean that. How about "Heaven-o." "Hell" and "Heaven" offer a definite choice. So why not "Heaven-o" and follow it with the person's name?

There is also "hell-bent," as so many are on so many subjects. Just think, if it were "heavenbent" we might all be better off.

And then there's "hellbroth," a brew claiming to work black magic. Wouldn't "heavenbroth" leave the participant not only gastronomically fulfilled but also spiritually fulfilled? It just might.

Get the Spelling Correct

The rookie police officer was cruising down the street, and came upon a dead dog. He picked up his phone, dialed the local pound and said,

"Ma'am, there's a dead dog lying out here in the middle of the street."

"What street, Officer?"

"It's in the 300 block of Wetickdahattchie."

"How do you spell that, Sir?"

"Just a minute, and I'll check."

When the officer came back to the phone he said, "It's Lee Street, L double e."

You May Be Excused

The public schools today--grammar, middle and high--
have many rules and regulations by which students are
expected to abide. In some respects, this is not totally unlike
the schools of yesteryear.

As a third-grader in a country school, with a teacher
who had taught my sister and three of my brothers, I came
along at a time when they were further streamlining the
scheduling and placing into effect better student compliance
with school policies.

One of those policies was that a student was not to be
excused during regular class time; any personal activity would
have to wait until the designated recess periods.

I remember, it was several days before the
Thanksgiving weekend, and I needed to use the bathroom. I
raised my hand for permission to speak and was recognized.

"Yes, Ramoth, what is it?"

"Miss Lina, may I be excused?"

"You know the new policy. Why do you want to be
excused?"

"I need to go to the bathroom."

"What is your problem, Ramoth?"

"I don't feel well in the stomach. Last night I was sick,
and now I have to go."

"How sick were you, Ramoth?"

I hesitated, and then said, "Well, very sick. Doctor
Garris came out to the house to see me."

"You may be excused to go to the bathroom."

* * *

Two days later my teacher came to our house to buy
her usual Thanksgiving turkey. (Mama always raised a dozen
or more hatchlings; it afforded her a little more Santa Claus

91

money.)

"Good afternoon, Miss Lina," said my mother as the teacher stepped from her car. (Everybody always called her "Miss Lina," although she was married and had grown daughters.)

"Hello, Mrs. Reese. I've come to pick up my turkey."

"Fine," said my mother. And the three of us began walking back toward the closed-in area where they were penned.

"Mrs. Reese, I was awfully sorry to hear about Ramoth's illness a few nights ago."

"What?" my mother said.

"Ramoth said he had been sick the night before and that Dr. Garris was out to the house to see him."

"Well, I don't know anything about that. I'll have a talk with him," said my mother.

Even before Miss Lina had finished her concern, I sensed bad news and had managed to fade from their company.

The turkey was caught, its feet tied, and then put in a toebag, with only its head and neck sticking out. They walked back to Miss Lina's car and put the turkey in the trunk. She paid mama, said goodbye and left.

"Ramoth?" my mother called.

"Yes, Mama," I said.

"Why did you tell Miss Lina that story?"

"Mama, I had to go to the bathroom, and under the new rules you can't except at recess time."

"But you told her that Doctor Garris was out here to see you that night, and you know that wasn't the truth. You were telling her a story, weren't you?"

"Yes."

"And you know you're not supposed to tell a story.

(Mama never felt comfortable using the word "lie," so the word "story" had two meanings: one positive, the other negative. A story that was read was an example of the positive meaning or application; and the other, which really meant telling a lie, had a negative connotation.)

It was at that time that I became quite sure that I was going to experience the final results for having told a story, and that the negative application was the one that was going to be used.

The switch I chose from the old tree was not too large and not to small, but the prolonged application thereof left me a little wiser. In the future I would confine the meaning of "story" to only its positive connotation, that of reading or being read to.

I never again asked Miss Lina for permission to be excused. Nature's calls were handled during the assigned recess periods.

The Search

Ol' Rabe had a reputation for making whiskey, and the Revenue boys, unannounced, called on him one day. They thoroughly searched the premises. After finding no signs of liquor, they began walking out, when one turned to the other and said, "Well, Ol' Rabe doesn't have any whiskey."

Ol' Rabe said, "Now wait just a minute, fellows. Don't you go out there and say that Ol' Rabe ain't got no whiskey; you'll hurt my business. You just tell them you couldn't find it."

It Can Happen

At a book signing while talking to me about the book on almanac gardening, a prospective buyer said that her husband was very familiar with the almanac and when he did get around to planting, he always referred to the farmer's almanac to get the right Moon sign to plant under. And then she added that he was such a couch potato he seldom got around to putting it to use.

"All he does," she said, "is watch television from morning 'til night."

And then she volunteered, "I'll tell you a funny incident that occurred. It wasn't funny then, but I laugh about it now.

"I decided that if the beans were ever going to get planted, I'd have to do it. So I went out to the garden one morning, without saying a word to him, planted them and returned to the house."

"Woman," he said, "where have you been?"

"I've been to the garden, and I planted the beans. If they were ever going to get planted, I had to do it. Once you get out of bed and up from the table, you don't budge from that couch."

"You're crazy," he said. "Don't you know that today the Moon is not in the right sign for planting beans. Ain't none of them going to do a thing."

And she said that he rasied such a ruckus with her that she just turned, walked up the stairs to her bedroom and cried, and prayed to the Lord that they would come up and grow bountifully.

"And how did they do?" I asked.

"Well, you know the Lord works in mysterious ways. We had the biggest crop of beans we've ever had."

Grandpa's Discovery

Family reunions are always a time for the relatives to meet, have fun, enjoy fine food, reminisce and brag. Each year my family's was held way out in the country on Grandpa's farm. The front yard was large and the huge oak trees offered the perfect shaded setting.

Temporary tables, made from boards, were erected between the trees, and the womenfolk covered them with tablecloths of various colors.

We ate, talked and laughed. Grandpa, a kind man, was not the most worldy, but he was loved by all. He enjoyed taking walks long before they became fashionable or had such acclaim by health enthusiasts.

At one reunion he decided he wanted to have a respite from all the activity, and so he decided to take a walk, alone, down the lane that led from the old home place out to the country road. Then he took an abandoned dirt bypass road that was no longer used by regular vehicular traffic. In fact, it had become known as "Lover's Lane."

And although Grandpa was the faithful father of eleven living children, when it came to preventative birth measures, he was completely unschooled. On this particular walk he found lying in Lover's Lane a discarded condom. Upon his return some of us learned of his find in a public way.

"Broadus," he asked of one of his married sons, "will you please tell me what in the world this is? I've never seen anything like it before." He held up the condon as it dangled between his thumb and forefinger.

My uncle, more versed in that field, took in the embarrassing situation at a glance, and said, "Papa, don't hold that up like that; put it down, put it down."

"But what is it?" grandpa insisted.

"Come with me, Papa, and I'll explain."

He put his arm around Grandpa and walked him around to the back of the house.

Now, none of us know, of course, exactly what Uncle Broadus said, or just how he explained the subject to Grandpa. But we have to assume that he was given a sufficient explanation.

There is one thing we do know, however, and whether it was due to Grandpa's age or to my uncle's enlightenment we'll never know, but Grandpa never had any more children.

To Each His Own

A stodgy but curious traveler stopped alongside the country road at a construction site, to inquire of one of the workers for directions. They spoke for a few moments and then the laid-back construction worker pulled out a plug of tobacco from his back pocket and offered to cut off a piece for the man.

"Oh, no!" said the traveler. "I'd rather go to a chicken house and rake up some of that to put in my mouth.

The worker took a chew from the plug, moved it around in his mouth a couple of times, and then finally packed it back in his left jaw. He hestitated for a moment, and then, in a slow southern drawl, said, "Well, I reckon it's all in what a fellow gets used to."

No License

The officer observed what appeared to be a very young kid driving a pickup truck loaded with wood. He pulled up behind him, turned on the blue light, and gently tapped the siren. Immediately the young fellow pulled over and stopped.

He approached the driver's door and asked for his license.

"I don't have a driver's license, sir. "

"You don't have a driver's license?"

"No, sir, I don't, and I've never had one."

"You look mighty young. How old are you?"

"I'm nine years old, but I've been driving since I was seven. My dad taught me how to drive then, and I've been helping him deliver wood ever since. I was going to deliver this load to Mrs. Minton, just a little farther up the road here. She's a real old lady, and she's nice, too. Daddy said she had called and wanted a load of wood right away."

"All right, son," said the officer. "But you're going to have to talk to the judge. I'll tell you what you do. You drive carefully on up to Mrs. Minton's--I know where that is--and I'll follow you. And then when you get there, you unload the wood. After that I want you to come with me, and we'll go down to the courthouse and you can talk to the Judge, and tell him what you have just told me. You just leave the pickup at Mrs. Minton's."

"All right, sir."

"What is your name?"

"My name is Robert, Robert Earl Collins."

"All right, Robert. Now when we get down to the courthouse, you go in and you tell the judge exactly what you were doing that caused me to stop you, and then tell him what you told me."

"I will, sir."

When they arrived at the Judge's chambers, the officer knocked on the door, slowly opened it, and motioned for the youngster to go in ahead of him.

The judge looked up from his desk and said, "Well, hello there, Robert. When are you going to bring my load of wood?"

The Phone Does Help

It was only the second day their new business had been open, and the husband and wife team were becoming worried no one was stopping in. And although they had purchased a phone and had it sitting on the desk in the reception room, the telephone company had not sent a man out to hook it up.

"Honey," the husband said, "if anyone comes in, just pretend you're busy taking appointments, or something like that."

Shortly afterwards, someone pulled up and came to the front door. Quickly, the wife picked up the phone and was faking a call when the man entered the reception area. He waited patiently.

"No, I'm sorry," the wife said. "He's booked up on Thursday morning. How about 3:00 or 4:00 on Thursday afternoon? Would that be satisfactory?

"All right, then, I'll put you down for 4:00 o'clock. And thank you. Goodbye."

She placed the dead phone on the hook, looked up and smiled at the gentleman and said, "Good morning and thank you for coming into our new offices. May I help you?"

"Yes, Ma'am, I'm from the phone company and I'm here to connect your phone."

The Silent Stones

A cousin bought an old country house that had been built several decades before. When she purchased the property, the realtor was totally up-front, and told her that the house was purported to have been built on top of a small abandoned cemetery, maybe about three or four grave sites.

"That doesn't bother me," said my cousin. "They're resting in peace, and so will I."

And with that having been said, there was no further mention of it. Several years passed and my cousin had to have two plumbers out to fix a problem she was having with the drainage system.

"Ma'am," said the older of the two men, "we'll have to get under the house and check it."

"Fine," she said, "go to it."

A few minutes later she heard a terrible knocking and bumping sound, and a few loud expletives. And both of the men came out from under the house breathing heavily.

"Ma'am," said the older, "did you know that this house is sitting on top of a cemetery? There are some old broken tombstones. One of them says, 'Here lies old John, the man who...' and I didn't take time to read the rest."

"Oh, yes," said my cousin, "but don't let that bother you; not a one of them will give you any difficulty."

"Ma'am, I'm sorry, but you'll have to get someone else to take care of this. I'm afraid of dead people."

And then he turned to his helper, who was shaking, and said, "Come on, Paul, let's get out of here. I think this place is haunted."

They ran to their pickup, threw their tools in the back and sped out of the lane, never to return again.

Remember

Maude and Ellie, both widowed, were longtime friends. They were strolling in Miami's Bayfront Park one afternoon.

"You know something, Ellie, I'm getting to the point I can't remember a thing, not a thing. I can't even remember what I had for lunch yesterday."

"At least that was yesterday," said Maude. "I can't remember what I had for breakfast this morning. But, tell me something, dear—and I hope you won't be offended when I ask you this—was it you or your sister who died last year?"

The Bean Lady

Shortly after presenting a radio program with my co-author of two books on gardening by the Moon signs, questions began to come in. One woman called and wanted to know if I had ever planted beans on the 1st day of May before speaking to anyone.

"No," I said, " I never have; and that is the first time I have ever heard that."

"Well," she said, "my father was very adamant about it. He wouldn't think of speaking to anyone, even my mother, on the 1st day of May until he went to the garden, planted the beans and then returned to the house."

"And you say then he would speak?"

"Oh, yes, just his good old self."

The Putdown/Pickup

The traveled tourist, a bit impressed with himself and his knowledge of the country, approached a mountain local and inquired about their goings-on.

"Say," he asked the local, "what in the world do you people do in the wintertime way up here in the mountains?"

"Oh, that's no problem at all," said the local. "We have plenty to do, and if you really want to know, I'll tell you."

"I do," said the tourist.

"Well, all winter long we just talk and laugh about the summer people."

The Evidence is Questionable

The young witness was being questioned by the judge.

"Young fellow, did you see that shot fired?"

"No, sir, I didn't, Your Honor, but I sure heard it."

"Well, you realize, of course, that type of evidence is inadmissible. You say you didn't see it but you heard it, is that right?"

"Yes, sir, that's right."

After further questioning the witness was told he could leave the court room, and as he turned and was walking out he began to laugh.

"Just a moment, young man," said the judge. "Come back up here to the bench."

"Yes, sir."

101

"As you were walking toward the door I heard you laughing."

"Yes, sir, I was, Your Honor. But did you see me laughing?"

"No, I didn't, but I certainly heard you."

"Well, Your Honor, isn't that the same kind of inadmissible evidence?"

Appreciation

Three mice died and went to heaven. After a few days St. Peter was making his goodwill rounds and inquired of their comfort.

The more vocal of the three spoke for all.

"St. Peter, we love it up here. The food is just wonderful, and everyone is so kind and generous."

"So you're okay, then, and you don't need anything?"

"No, not really," said the spokesmouse, "but there is one thing that would help us, and I'm almost embarrassed to mention it."

"No, no, don't hesitate, " said St. Peter. "Go right ahead. We want you to be happy up here."

"Well," said the spokesman, "it would certainly help us if we could each get a pair of skates. You see, this place is so beautiful that we love to run around all day and enjoy it. But it is so vast, and we have such short legs, that we do get tired. You know, the place is really big. And if we could each have a pair of skates, it would be just great."

"You certainly may," offered St. Peter, "and we'll get them for you right away."

The three were outfitted with skates and having a grand time, enjoying their new easy method of maneuvering.

A few weeks later two cats died and also went to Heaven. Shortly thereafter St. Peter approached and asked if there was anything he could do to make their stay more enjoyable.

"St. Peter," the male cat said, "we couldn't ask for better conditions. It is just wonderful, and we especially like the Meals on Wheels."

I Just Don't Feel Well

Only a few youngsters have not played sick to avoid school. At eight, I was no exception.

"Mama," I said, "I don't feel well."

"What's wrong?"

"I don't know. I just don't feel right."

"Well, you go and tell your daddy and see what he says."

My father listened, and said, "All right, I hear you. Maybe I should take you to see Dr. Garris. But if you think you'll get to feeling better, I'll just take you on to school."

"I'll go to the doctor." After all, how would he know whether I was or wasn't sick?

The doctor listened to my explanation, took my blood pressure and pulse, and said, "I think I know your problem."

He took out a bottle of white pills from his desk drawer. "Take two when you get home, with water, and then go to bed. Afterwards, take one every two hours for the rest of the day, and by tomorrow morning I think you will feel better."

As we were returning home I asked, "Daddy, what kind of pills are these that he gave me?"

"Son, I don't know, but Dr. Garris is a good doctor, and if you just take them and follow his advice, I'm sure you'll be okay tomorrow."

As we were pulling in the driveway, I said, "Daddy, I don't know why, but already I'm feeling better."

"Good," he said, "that's fine, but the pills and bed rest will do the trick, and mama will bring you a pill every two hours, so let's go ahead with Dr. Garris' orders."

After that episode, I never again missed school because "I just don't feel right."

The Emergency

The country doctor was loved by all in the community, and for years he had served them well in the small town. Although he was the only doctor within miles, he never took advantage of that fact, and treated all his patients alike, always being reasonable and fair when it came to charges. A person's station in life in the small town made no difference to him; he was a messenger with a message, and all thought he delivered it well.

One evening just after he and his wife had gone to bed, the phone rang. It was the husband of one of his patients. The man said that his wife was having labor pains more frequently, and wanted the doctor to come to the house in case it became necessary to deliver the baby. There was no hospital in the town.

Quickly, the doctor dressed and said to his wife, "I'll be

back as soon as I can, but you never know about these types of calls." He had been gone only a minute or so when his wife phoned her "gentleman caller," and shortly thereafter her lover rushed over. He walked upstairs and joined her. A little more than an hour had passed when the wife heard a noise downstairs, and then a sound of the front door being opened.

"Quick," she said, "you've got to hide or do something. That's my husband returning from the house call for that pregnant woman. I didn't know he was going to get back so soon."

Her husband began walking up the stairs, and the gentleman caller could not escape via the door, so he quickly raised the window, jumped out from the second story.

"Help, help," he yelled. "I've broken my leg. Help me."

The doctor heard the commotion, stepped into the bedroom and saw his wife lying in bed.

"What's going on?" he asked. The wife did not answer. And when he saw the window open and heard a groan, he walked over, looked down and saw the young man on the ground. Without saying another word to his wife, he ran downstairs, went outside and approached the injured fellow.

"Damn you," he said, "I ought to let you lie there and suffer."

"Doctor, I'm hurting. Help me, help me. I think this leg is broken."

"Yes, I know, and you deserved it. You stay there and I'll back my car around and take you down to the office. I shouldn't do a thing, but I'm the only doctor around, and my Hippocratic Oath compels me to help you. Damn you."

Now, just how good a job the doctor did on splinting the leg is not known, but it would seem the temptation would be great to do something a little less than would normally be expected. But then, the Oath is not to be taken lightly, and so one has to presume that the gentleman caller did have the use of that leg fully restored.

As to the problem between the doctor and his wife, we don't know. Maybe he extended the same tenets of the Hippocratic Oath to their relationship, thus successfully splinting it, too.

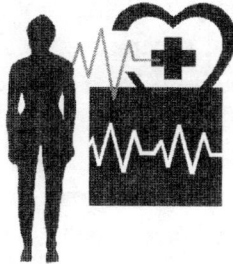

Lucky Tiger Shampoo

Times are not what they used to be. I well remember my Junior year in high school. In order to put an extra nickel in my pocket, I applied for a clerk's job and was accepted at one of the local general stores in the small town where I lived. I was to work all day on Saturdays, which meant from 7 in the morning until closing at 10 in the evening.

My job was to learn the art of serving customers, and doing it with a smile, to give them what they wanted, as long as they had the money to pay for their purchases. The store was owned by an older gentleman who knew everybody in town and for miles around.

My pay for the Saturday work would be 75 cents. That was fine with me. Every nickel helped back then when a nickel was a nickel.

During the week before I got there on one of those Saturdays, a salesman called on my boss and sold him on stocking a new product called Lucky Tiger Hair Tonic and Shampoo. It came in two separate bottles. They were held together in a heavy cardboard wrapper, with only the upper half of the glass bottles showing.

My boss opened one of the bottles and showed it to me when I came on duty. The aroma was pleasing, and I wanted to purchase a set. So when the time came to settle up that night, hoping he would be generous, I told him to take out the price of one of the Lucky Tiger sets and just pay me the difference. The set sold for 49 cents.

I had read him wrong. He opened the cash drawer, and holding the Lucky Tiger carton in one hand, he reached in, took out 26 cents, and handed both to me, and said, "I hope it works for you. I think you're getting a good buy."

It was a lesson well learned, and a hair/shampoo tonic purchase hard earned.

Malphus Williams' Weekly Allowance

It was at the same general store during my Junior year that another experience occurred. I was left in charge of the store during the lunch hour. Malphus Williams and his wife were two of the poorer black tenants who lived on a wealthy family's large farm. The farmer had pre-arranged with my boss to allow Malphus to shop there on credit. The landowner would periodically come in and "settle up," as they used to say.

The limit, however, that Malphus could buy each week--usually on a Saturday--was $5.00, and only in groceries.

I remember clearly one particular Saturday when he came while the boss was out to lunch. We talked for a brief period and then he began to order groceries.

"Give me a 10-pound bag of flour, and a five-pound bag of sugar and some cheese, the sharp kind."

"How about some of these dried beans?" I asked.

"Yep," he said, "two pounds of them there ones," he said, pointing, "and one of them. And a box of those Moon Pies, and some of them Pepsi-Colas. And don't forget my Brown Mule chewing tobacco," he added.

I willingly obliged and was pleased to have made the sale, although I was keeping close watch on the amount involved. With the purchase of the tobacco, it brought him within three cents of his $5.00 allowance.

"Malphus," I said, "you've got three cents left."

"Then just give me some of them Mary Jane candies there in the case."

I fished out three cents worth, put his groceries in the bags. He put them in his cart, got in and said to his trusty old mule, "Giddy up there, Maudie." And away he went down the road.

It was only a couple of minutes afterwards that the boss came in and inquired as to who had been in. When I told him that Malphus had and spent his $5.00 limit, he asked what he had purchased.

"He got a 10-pound bag of flour, some sugar, cheese and some dried beans--two different kinds, I believe--and a big box of Moon pies and some Pepsi-Colas. And then he had three cents left, so he took it in Mary Jane candy. Here's the list I made."

"Oh, no," said my boss; "he's not supposed to have some of that stuff. He can't buy Moon Pies and Pepsi-Colas. I have on file here the things that he can buy with the $5.00, and he can't go outside of that. It is staples only, none of that fancy stuff."

"I'm sorry."

"That's okay," he said, "I should have told you, but I never thought of it. I'll take care of it."

He jumped in his car, took off down the road and overtook Malphus and Maudie. In just a few minutes he returned. Malphus came up later in his cart.

He turned in his Moon pies and Pepsi-Colas and the three cents worth of Mary Janes, and then was given an appropriate amount of other staples to round out his $5.00 limit.

"Be sure the next time he comes in that he limits it to the items on this list. I keep it right here behind the cash drawer."

"Yes, sir, I will."

The following Saturday when he came in, Malphus stayed within the $5.00 limit. I am sure he knew all along what he was supposed to buy, but he took advantage of the situation and, for a time at least, probably felt good about it.

Opportunity

The young boy handed his application to the farmer.

"Your references certainly look all right, for a job here in our poultry yard."

"Well, sir, is there any opportunity to rise?"

"You bet there is," replied the farmer. "You'll rise at four o'clock every morning."

Maybe Later

While empanelling a jury for a highly publicized case, both counsel for the plaintiff and the defendant were trying to elicit information that would enable them to seat jurors that they thought would be unbaised.

"Sir," asked the plaintiff's attorney, "you realize this case is a very emotional one, for both the wife and the husband seated over here at these two tables?"

"Yes, sir, I do."

"And we may need to ask you some questions that you might consider personal, but we hope that you will come forth with truthful answers. I know you will."

"Yes, sir."

"Mr. Brown, do you own a home?"

"Yes, sir, I do."

"Are you married or single?"

"I am married, sir. I have been for three years."

"Have you formed or expressed an opinion in this matter?"

"No, sir, I have not, not in three years. That's really not long enough."

Signatures

While book-signing with the co-author of two books on using the almanac for planting, harvesting, and many other activities around the household, a lady of years approached and looked through both books.

"I'll take them both," she said. "And if you will, on that one, just autograph it. But on this one, autograph and also put an inscription."

"Do you have something special that you would like me to write in for you?"

"Yes, I do," she said. "Put in, 'This wonderful book on planting and harvesting is for Alicia, Mabel, Byron, Jean, Pauline, Richard, Erick and Tony.'"

I was beginning to run out of space when she said "Tony."

"You've got quite a few there, Ma'am."

"Yes," she said, "and you see that last one there, 'Tony?'"

"I do, yes."

"Well, he is my little three-year old grandson, and when he gets big enough to read, he'll realize his grandmother 'won't' crazy."

Hairy Advice

"Had you come to me when you first started to lose your hair, I could have told you how to save it," the barber said to the balding middle-ager.

"Well, what would you have told me?" asked the man.

"To put it in a shoe box and put the box in your dresser drawer," replied the barber.

Something New

"Hey, look at that fancy job," said the man to his nearby neighbor, when the neighbor drove up in a shiny new pickup.

"Thank you. I just got it yesterday for my wife. And now I'm thinking about selling my children."

Be Kind

I was griping about the rabbits eating my garden, and the neighbor, always a kind and thoughtful soul, said, "Well, just remember this. They may not be as intelligent as humans, but they are as determined in their ways—about as much, I expect—as the other inhabitants of this area."

The Bookstore

The older man was browsing through a second-hand book store, and found one that had been signed by a well-known author.

He approached the unschooled proprietor and asked about the price.

"Well," he said, "it's secondhand, as you see, and I had priced it at 75 cents, but some SOB has written his name in it, so I'll let you have it for a quarter."

Word Definitions

The teacher asked her students to think of words that might be challenging to other classmates. And when they finished that exercise, the teacher said, "All right, I'll ask one now.

"Charles, my word is 'recuperate.' Think of that word now. I guess your father goes to work every day?"

"Yes, he does."

"And when he finishes working, is he tired?"

"Yes, ma'am, he is."

"And then when night comes what does he do?"

"That's what my mother wants to know."

Education Pays

After listening to the professor (whose last name was the same as mine, Reese) give the banquet address at a writers' conference, I approached him to express my appreciation for his having come to speak before our group. I told him that his message was a vital one for all writers, and that the humor he used in putting over his points was unparalleled.

"Thank you, thank you very much," he said.

And then I reminded him that as great as the Reeses were, who spell their name with an "s," that there were quite a number who spell it with a "c."

"Oh, yes," he quipped, "those are the illiterate ones."

Pharmaceutical Assistance

The doctor moved into a new neighborhood, and in an effort to welcome him, one of the neighbors decided to invite other neighbors and him for dinner.

She didn't send a formal invitation, with an R.S.V.P. It was just a friendly note. She thought it would be part of letting him know that they were all friendly people in the area.

Very shortly thereafter she received a reply. It was written in typical doctor's writing, and the host to-be could not decipher it.

She showed it to another neighbor who mentioned that only pharmacists can read a doctor's writing.

So the host took it to her local drug store and asked for help.

"The doctor sent this to me and I don't know what it says."

"Let's see if we can help you."

The druggist took it, went into the back room for a few minutes and returned with a bottle, and said, "There you are, ma'am. That will fix you right up."

A Debt Repaid

In olden days, many things were handled differently. I remember, quite clearly, as a pre-teenager, of wanting to save money. So much so that often when I earned a nickel or dime in whatever manner, I had a penchant for holding back a portion of it for "a rainy day," as my parents termed it.

At one stage of her life my grandmother dipped snuff, and she gave me one of her used snuff boxes.

I took the box, put in the few pennies I had, closed it, and then buried it in the backyard behind the chicken house. Subsequently, each time I acquired money, I would carefully remove the box from the hole, put a portion of the money in and rebury it.

As I was walking to town one day (a mile from our house), I stopped and spoke with people who lived along the road. One of them was a delightful elderly black woman we called "Aunt Mary." She had often helped my mother with the heavier household duties, and when my mother was ready to deliver my two younger brothers she was right there for a few days each time.

She would kid me about my buried investment, but only my mother knew where it was buried. (Always mindful of tomorrow, I thought someone should know in the event of my untimely death.)

Years passed; I grew into a teenager, graduated from high school and attended business college. After that there was a two-year period in which I worked with the Navy Department, and then Uncle Sam called me for service during World War II.

I served more than three years in the Service. When I was discharged I returned to visit my old home town. One of the people I especially wanted to see was "Aunt Mary."

As I walked up her steps, knocked on the door, an older woman than I remembered entered the hallway, walked up to the front screen door and stared.

"Aunt Mary, do you remember me?"

After a moment's hesitation, she stretched out the bony arms of her frail body, leaned forward and embraced me, and said, "Son, do you still bury your money?"

We laughed, and she invited me to join her on the porch. I sat in the swing while she rocked in the chair that was obviously where she spent much of her time.

Each of us told the other of our life since we had last met.

After we had spent nearly two hours together, I rose to say goodbye, and as I reached for her hand, she again embraced me, started laughing, and then said, "You were too much in your day, son, and you still owe me that dime you borrowed one day when you were walking to town. Let me know if you have not dug up all your money; I can use it right about now."

It was obvious that she was telling the truth. I took out a ten dollar bill, handed it to her. She thanked me, and then, as I was walking down the steps, she said, "Don't forget the snuff box. Your mama told me where you buried it."

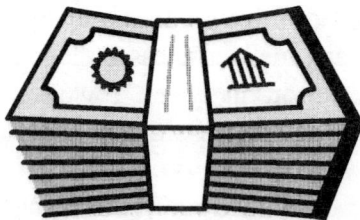

The Loaded Bullet

Numerous crops were grown on our farm, and one of them was cotton. It was before the days of the mechanical picker, so it had to be picked by hand. When it was ready for picking, daddy would always hire additional help. One of those was a dark woman we called "Aunt Darthoolie." She would always bring her youngest children with her, and they would play up and down the rows as she picked cotton.

On this occasion it was her two girls, four and five, that she brought. And although I was young and could offer my father little help as far as picking cotton was concerned, I did play around in the field. On one of the occasions, Aunt Darthoolie said, "Ramoth, I will give you this if you will kiss Claramae." She was the older of her two children.

I looked at the cartridge and saw that it was just like the ones daddy used in his 22 rifle. Although I had had little experience in the art of kissing, it seemed a fair exchange.

And so I told Aunt Darthoolie that I would.

"Claramae," she called, "come here. Ramoth wants to kiss you."

The two of us stood close, and I leaned over and gave her a peck on the cheek.

"No, no," said Aunt Darthoolie, "not there. Do it on the lips."

I did, and although Claramae didn't object, she didn't act excited, but Aunt Darthoolie did. "That's nice," she said. "Here, take the bullet, and remember where it came from."

Once everyone had finished picking for the day and I returned to the house, I showed mama the bullet.

"Where did you get that?"

"Aunt Darthoolie gave it to me."

"She gave it to you?"

"Yes."

"Where did she get it?"

"I don't know."

"Why did she give it to you?"

"Well, she said if I would kiss Claramae I could have it."

"And you kissed her?"

"Yes."

"You ought to be ashamed of yourself."

"Mama, it didn't hurt. And look, I have a bullet for daddy's rifle."

My mother walked into the living room, looked on the mantel, and the usual box of bullets was missing. When daddy came in, she asked him if he had moved it.

"No, I didn't."

"Well, then" mama said, "I think I know where the bullet came from that Ramoth brought in from the field."

"From the field?" my father asked.

"Yes. Darthoolie gave it to him for kissing Claramae."

My father did not appear to be a bit disturbed. In fact, with a knowing smile on his face, he looked over at my mother and said, "Don't worry; maybe it's good experience for him."

The Budding Attorney

My friend was married to a young attorney. While he was trying to get established she did much of his legal work at home, including typing from his dictation various legal documents and letters.

They had a son in the second grade. He was exposed to much of the legal jargon, and often listened to some of his father's recorded dictation. In addition, the wife would read aloud from some of the documents.

This exposure to the legal atmosphere at home rubbed off on the young boy. When the teacher would call on her students to tell stories that they had heard and wanted to talk about, the youngster would raise his hand, stand and begin his story with:

"Whereas, and therefore on this day, we, the parties, do agree..." and then he would continue, weaving in his story.

The teacher was quite impressed, and later in the week she asked him to give a speech on his father's profession.

He rose from his desk, stood erect and said, "Well, Whereas and therefore, the parties come before this court on this day, and offer-- No, that isn't right. The party of the first part will give to the party of the second part all of his property for the favors herein listed." And then he proceeded to tell things about his father.

When he had finished, the teacher thanked him and asked that he be seated.

He sat, looked her straight in the eye and asked, "Miss Brown, if it pleases the Court, could we have the verdict?"

The Aging Gent

He had no reason to suspect old age,
Except chronologically.
Not even one who called himself a sage
Could see it biologically.

But then the elements of time and space
Began to creep upon the scene.
They forced themselves, though left no trace,
Just asked that he remain as keen.

The Fair Warning

The young man had been subpoenaed to give his deposition as a witness in a case involving the disappearance of two automobiles from a car dealership. He ignored the subpoena and had to be picked up by the local sheriff and brought to the courthouse for the taking of the deposition.

He was placed under oath by the court reporter, and then questioned by the respective attorneys.

Once they had finished their questioning and the deposition was concluded, the attorney who had subpoenaed him said, "Sir, I appreciate you giving us your testimony under oath here today and I am sorry it had to be under such unpleasant circumstances, you know, sending the sheriff out to bring you in."

The young man remained silent, rose from his chair, walked to the door, and then turned and said, "Well, let me tell you something: You'd better not subpoena me again because the next time I'll tell the truth."

.Salesmanship

The gracious lady had raised her family, watched them marry and have children, and for years had enjoyed the rewards of having grandchildren. Now she was older and lived with one of her daughters, and her mind was becoming less agile. She was more forgetful and more vulnerable to the everyday exposures that constantly bombarded the public through TV sales pitches and door-to-door salesmen.

While watching the Evening News on the local station, the salesman for one of the area's largest automobile dealerships was right there with his message.

In his usual showy style, he stood beside a bright red Chevrolet and pointed to its various exterior features. "Just look at this beautiful automobile. It is a work of art. Look at these graceful lines. Notice how all the exterior features blend one into the other. It's the car for you. It is one that you will enjoy, one that you will be proud to drive."

And then he extended his right hand and index finger toward the TV audience and said, "You, you sitting out there right now, this car is for you. All you have to do tomorrow morning is come down and drive it away. Come on down, we'll save it for you."

As soon as the news was over, her daughter called: "Mother, come on in, dinner is ready."

She rose, walked slowly to the table, sat down and began to eat. Midway through the meal she asked, "What are you doing tomorrow morning?"

"Well, Mother, I was going to do some laundry. Why? Do you have something in mind you'd like to do?"

" Yes. You know Charlie, the man that talks about the Chevrolets?"

"Yes, I know who you mean."

121

"Well, tonight he brought out a beautiful red Chevrolet, and he turned right around and pointed toward me and said, 'Now, we've got the car for you.' And then he said all I had to do was come down tomorrow morning and he'd fix me right up. He said I could drive it back home. Can't we go down and get it?"

"Oh, I see," said the daughter. "Well, mother, why don't we just wait and see how things go tomorrow. Is that all right?"

"Yes, but he did point straight at me; and he said it was my car, and I think we should go down and get it. I'd hate to lose it."

"Well, mother, we'll talk about it at the breakfast table."

"All right."

Morning came but no mention was made of the beautiful red automobile.

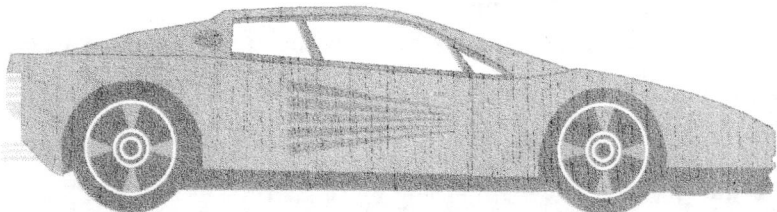

A Real Vacation

The judge, with a reputation for a good sense of humor, called both counsel to the Bench to discuss a matter.

"Counsel," he said, "I hope that you fellows can move this case along this morning because my vacation starts this afternoon."

"But, Your Honor, three months ago this was set as a two-day case, and Your Honor's calendar, I believe, will reflect that I am correct on that."

The other counsel said, "Judge, my colleague here is right, and both of us have subpoenaed our witnesses to begin coming in later this morning and then throughout the afternoon and a part of tomorrow. This comes as a complete surprise."

"It certainly does," said the other counsel. "And, Judge, may I ask--and I realize it may be personal--but why has this been changed from a two-day case to just a half-day case?"

"Gentlemen, don't fret," said the judge, with a grin on his face. "It is my vacation. You see, I just put my wife on the plane for England this morning at 8 o'clock, and she'll be gone for two weeks."

Try It

While reporting a meeting comprised of selected salesmen for the Bible and other religious publications, the chairman introduced each of them, and then said that Francis Bonaventure de Sales, who was born in 815, was deemed the perfect writer of the 16th century.

"He was a religious thinker. And in 1925 Pope Pius declared him 'The Heavenly Patron Saint of All Writers, St. Francis de Sales.'"

And then she continued, "Some say he wrote more than Shakespeare. I don't know whether or not that is accurate, but he did write a publication titled 'Introduction to a Devout Life.' The following is attributed to him, and I would remind all of the speakers here today to keep it in mind:

"The more you say, the less people will remember."

Gregariousness

Gregariousness is nothing more than
overt ignorance operating
in an acceptably obvious manner.

Talent

While friends and I were visiting in New Orleans on Bourbon Street, we saw many artists displaying their wares and talents. One was particularly amusing.

One of my friends approached the gentle looking middle-aged fellow, who was strumming on his guitar, and asked if he would play a particular song.

"I can't play that," he said.

"Well," my friend asked, "what can you play?"

"I can play two songs: one of them is 'Dixie' and one of them ain't."

The Shoes

Miss Sally was nearly seventy and still a spinster. She had been a registered nurse during her career days, and was loved by all the townspeople. Often she was kidded about her marital status, and was never at a loss for words when someone tried to jokingly razz her about it.

She was visiting in our home, and my father asked her if she intended to ever marry. Quick as a flash, she retorted.

"Tom," she said, "no man will ever put his shoes under my bed."

Lafayette

The wealthy middle-aged couple were before the judge for a final hearing in their divorce after many years of marriage.

Counsel for the husband and counsel for the wife had worked out all the details, including agreement on who was to get what property, along with their many other assets, but the one thing neither party was willing to agree on was which one should have Lafayette, their French Poodle.

"Your Honor, I think my colleague here will agree with me on this issue. We have both spent a great amount of time trying to work this out with our clients, and we must confess we have not been able to resolve it. Neither one of them will budge; each of them wants Lafayette."

"Well," said the judge to the couple, "I am sure both of you are very devoted to your pet. I've seen pictures of Lafayette, and he is truly a beautiful dog."

"He is, Your Honor," said the wife. "He is one of the family. And he considers me his mother. As you know, we never had children; Lafayette is our child. He's ten years old and still in good health."

"I don't want to make this decision," said the judge, "and I'll tell you what I'm going to do.

"I'm pleased that you both have been able to agree on all the other items listed, and I commend you for that. And, counsel, you both deserve much credit.

"What I would like for you to do now, though, is go outside in the hall, each with your attorney, and see if you can't come to some decision. Give it another try. I just don't want to have to make this decision. You are both emotional about the issue, and I can understand that.

"So, if you will, Counsel, each of you take your client

outside, take a few minutes and try one more time to see if you can't resolve the matter."

The parties were out for nearly 20 minutes and returned to the judge's chambers.

"Your Honor," said Counsel for the husband, "we have been unable to come to an agreement. My client feels he is entitled to Lafayette and--"

The other counsel interrupted, "And mine feels she is entitled to him, Your Honor."

"All right," said the judge. "I hate to have to do this, but you have left me no choice."

And then he looked toward the wife and said, "I am going to grant joint custody. You get Lafayette for three months, and then he gets custody for three months.

"I wish you both, and Lafayette, much happiness in the future."

Often in Aging

**The older men become
The faster they succumb
To acting like "the boys"
Who have a bunch of toys.**

Prison Time

Three elderly relatives who live in the flat country, over near the Outer Banks of North Carolina, were visiting in my home in the western part of the state, the beautiful mountain area. I was driving them around the countryside and had shown them where Johnny (of the famous ballad "Frankie & Johnny") was buried.

We then drove up to Mount Mitchell (the highest peak east of the Mississippi), back down, and were driving through McDowell County. A few miles out of the town of Marion is a State prison, and as they looked over and saw some of the prisoners in the yard ambling around, they inquired about the place.

I gave them general information on the prison and then, with a hesitancy in my voice, said, "I have a confession to make."

"What's that?" one of the cousins asked.

"Well, at this stage in my life I'm really neither proud nor ashamed to admit this, but I have spent time in that prison."

"What!" one of them exclaimed. "You mean in that prison?"

"Yes, right there. You're looking at it."

"You haven't, really, have you?"

"Yes, I have," I said. "And, to tell you the truth, you are the first to know about it. I've never mentioned it to a soul in the family. But, as I said, I am neither proud nor ashamed."

Another of the cousins spoke up. "Ramoth, I can't believe it. What happened? What did you do?"

"Well, I'll give it to you straight. None of us is perfect, and I was there for three hours."

"For what?" the third cousin quickly inquired.

"You're going to have to accept my word for it when I tell you that I was with two others, two attorneys, no less. You see, the three of us were in there to take the depositions of two of the inmates, and I was the court reporter."

Barber Shop Wisdom

"My first wife said that after a man reaches 40, they ought to do him like they do a horse when he gets that age."

"What's that?" I asked.

"Take him out in the woods and shoot him."

"That sounds similiar to something my wife said," offered one of the gentlemen waiting to have his hair cut.

"She said, 'After a man is 40 he has no more business being out of the ground than a mole.'"

Reciprocity

During his grandmother's last days she told her daughter she wanted to be buried in her favorite tailored suit, a light blue with pearl buttons.

She then looked over at her grandson and said, "I hope you win the lottery."

He said, "Well, Grandma, when you get up there send me the lucky number."

Quick as a flash she retorted, "I will, and don't forget to send some back up."

It Does Make A Difference

I had moved into the mountain area and made friends with many of the neighbors. I was told before moving in that "outsiders" never become "insiders," and that you have to be born "on the soil," as it were, or else you're forever destined to be "one of those" from somewhere else. I would later learn whether or not this was an accurate assessment of the good mountain people.

As time passed, I became especially fond of a fiercely independent woman. She was in her early 80s, born and raised on the very land she was then standing on at the time we were "exchanging the day." I admired her spunk, her forthrightness, and the apparent goodness she exuded each time we spoke.

She had lived--or so I was told--a good life, but at times a hard life. She and her husband had many children, all now long since grown, married, and some of them with grandchildren of their own.

Word came one day that my elderly neighbor had become ill and was in the local hospital. Because I admired this woman's spirit and appreciated her sense of humor and determination, I immediately drove to the hospital to visit her.

"Hello there," I said, as I stepped inside her room.

"Good morning," she said, a bit slowly, and I am sure it was from her weakened condition, because normally she was strong of voice.

"Woman," I asked, "what in the world are you doing in this place? The last time I saw you you were out in the yard working in your flowers."

"Well," she answered, "it's like this: They tell me these doctors know what they're doing. I'm not totally convinced that they do, but I'll soon find out. And if they don't, then there's little I can do, 'cause I certainly don't know what's ailing me. All I know is, I don't like hospitals."

And then she looked over at the patient in the only other bed in the room, and said to her, "Have you met this young man? He's my neighbor."

"No, I haven't," she said.

"Mr. Reese, this is Marybelle Robinson, and Marybeile, this is Mr. Reese."

We exchanged nods and said hello, after which the roommate asked my neighbor, "Is he one of us?"

My good neighbor answered, "No, he ain't, but he's a mighty nice fellow."

So, you see, having been born in North Carolina doesn't automatically entitle you to become, or ever be, "one of us."

It Has Its Advantages

Old age has many disadvantages, but when
      you put them beside the advantages, they
      often fade into the background.
And, as one humorous senior said, "Don't ever
      underestimate old age; it's the only time in
      life when you can sing while you brush
      your teeth."

After Awhile

Once I could get by on looks;
And then I relied on charm.
I'm older now, minus wisdom,
So you can understand my alarm

Maybe

The old gent constantly griped about paying taxes, remarking that they increase each year.

"Dear Lord," he prayerfully asked, "will I have to pay them up there, too?"

He got no message from above, and so the next day he tried again.

"Dear Lord, yesterday I asked, most respectfully, if I would have to continue paying taxes once I get up there, and I didn't get an answer."

"Well," said the voice from above, "The Great One is checking, so if you will just be patient and have faith, I'm sure He'll come through with an answer."

The following morning when he arose, the old gent knelt beside his bed and began his morning ritual of thanking the Lord and repeating the same question.

Finally, a voice was heard: "Your status is in question. It is not whether or not you will pay taxes up here; it is whether or not your final residence will be up here."

A Fact

As a court reporter for many years, I was afforded the opportunity to work with many in the legal profession.

One of the judges with whom I often served as court reporter was quite down-to-earth in his approach to life--a spade was a spade, no ifs, ands or buts. And on his chambers' wall hung a number of pictures, but one large one in particular I will never forget.

It was almost life-size, taken of him shortly after he was born, he said. The picture showed him lying face down in an old-fashioned pair of scales like the country stores used in weighing out the merchandise. In this picture, he was clothed only in newborn innocence, and his tiny chubby face was turned toward the front. Just beside, but within the same frame, and of the same proportion, was a picture of the setting sun. The caption underneath was:

"FROM OBSCURITY TO OBLIVION"

Seldom did an attorney come before him on chamber matters that comments on the picture were not made. And he would always enlighten them about the circumstances, and then end the conversation by calling to their attention the fact that we come in with nothing and we take nothing with us when we leave.

"Just try," he would say, "to work toward being the best in the profession."

"You're right," said one of the attorneys before him.

And the the judge quickly added, with a twinkle in his eye, "Of course, that is more difficult for some of us than it is for others."

Comfort Is Everything

While working as a court reporter in the State of Florida many of the cases up for trial or hearing were routine, some moreso than others, and many had their elements of humor.

At the era in which this occurred, a furniture manufacturer made a sofa/bed which they called a "Castro Convertible." The quality and beauty were outstanding, and it became extremely popular.

The store in this particular locale used both the TV and newspaper to advertise the beauty, comfort and style of the sofa/bed. At times a picture would be shown on TV with a customer sitting on the sofa and then another shot showing the sofa in its open bed position, with the customer relaxing luxuriously on the neatly made-up bed.

And although the furniture in question played no part whatsoever in the following case, it did come into the picture, indirectly and probably improperly.

The hearing was set to have the judge hear testimony from the Plaintiff, a beautiful woman, who had sued for divorce from a prominent South Florida professional. Her own reputation was well-known far and wide. In earlier days, prior to her marriage, she had been employed as a "lady of service," or as some would bluntly say, a high-priced "call girl."

At the scheduled hour, counsel for both parties appeared in the courtroom, along with the court reporter and judge.

"Counsel," asked the judge, "where is your client?"

"Your Honor, I expected her here. I spoke with her from her home about an hour and a half ago. She said she would be here. So I am sure she'll be along momentarily. I'm sorry for the delay."

The judge was quite stern. He ran a tight court, always prompt in starting his hearings and trials on time, and expected counsel and their clients to be on time. So, he wasn't too pleased with the delay of the wife.

He waited several more minutes, then stood and told counsel he was going to his chambers to do some work and asked that they let him know when she arrived.

Another fifteen minutes elapsed and still the plaintiff did not show. It was at this time the judge re-entered the courtroom, sat at the Bench and asked, "Counsel, what have you found out about your client? We've only set aside an hour for this hearing and nearly 30 minutes of that has passed."

"Your Honor, I don't know. I am embarrassed. I suppose she has been held up in traffic or something. I am very sorry. I called her home again and there was no answer, so I presume she is en route."

The judge, showing his impatience, asked, "How was she coming down here, by bus or car, or do you know?"

Before her lawyer could answer, counsel for the husband spoke up and said, "Probably by Castro Convertible, Your Honor."

Shampoo

I used to shampoo my hair
And comb it every day.
Time aborted that routine,
Affording me no say.

135

The Bean Story

Grandpa plowed the garden rows, all perfectly straight. He then put high sticks with pieces of different-colored streamers, made from leftover scrap material Grandma had used to make quilts, to show what each row would have planted in it. He always had his own method of marking, and kept a chart. The material that was primarily yellow was used to denote yellow squash; red, for beets; green gingham, snap beans; just plain green was for cucumbers, and so on.

"Son," he said to my Uncle Broadus, "I've got to go to town with your mother. I'm going to leave these seeds for you to plant in those two rows over there with the green gingham markers. They're bush beans, so you need to plant them about 4 inches apart, and put a couple or three in each hill. No more than that."

"Yes, sir."

Uncle Broadus waited until he was sure Grandpa had left for town, and then decided it was not necessary to put just two or three in each hole. If he put more, he could finish a lot earlier and return to playing with Jeremiah, the goat.

So, he proceeded to dig little holes with his hand, and instead of dropping two or three, he dropped 7 or 8. As a result, he barely had enough to finish one of the two rows Grandpa had set aside for beans.

Grandpa returned from town and asked, "Did you get the beans planted?"

"Yes, sir, I sure did. It didn't take me long, either. I only had enough for one row."

"What?" Grandpa asked. "I was sure there was enough there for two rows, or pretty near it. We'll just wait and see."

Within a few weeks, the beans sprouted, and everyone

of them must have come through because each hill had seven or eight young tender plants.

"Son," Grandpa said, "I know now why you didn't have enough seed to plant both rows. You know I told you to put 2 or 3 in each hill, not 7 or 8."

"Yes, sir."

"Come on over here to this tree, and we'll take care of that problem."

He did, with a switch cut from the tree at the end of the row. And although Uncle Broadus had many occasions to plant seeds after that, he never again put more in a hill than he was told.

The Culinary Test

The newlyweds had just moved into their beautifully furnished apartment and were getting squared away.

The husband came home from work to a fresh-cooked meal, and when he bit down on the cake, he said, "Honey, what's wrong. It has a gritty taste to it."

"Well, the recipe calls for two eggs. I guess I didn't get the shells beaten fine enough."

The Dulcimer Ladies

While autographing books at an annual festival reminiscent of the olden days, three elderly ladies, dressed in the appropriate garb for the occasion, were seated outside the entrance to the building in which we were signing.

They had their dulcimers and were playing some of the oldtimey favorites.

"Say," I asked, "what were the names of the last two pieces you just played?"

"Oh," said one of them, "the first one was 'Gail's Jolly Jig,' and the other one"--and she hesitated a moment and another one of them said, "It was 'Whiskey Before Breakfast.' Try it; you'll like it."

The Wise Old Maller

While seated in the Mall waiting for my friend to finish shopping, an elderly gentleman sat down beside me, and we began to talk. Just a few feet away a Lion's Club member was offering free preliminary eye examinations.

We both had our eyes examined and conversed about that. And then he began to tell me he suffered from diverticulitis.

"I'll tell you," he said, "the stomach today is just not built to last as long as we live."

The Surprise or Shock

"Oh, my, look at that," said my friend to her neighbor as they stepped inside the country store. She was pointing down the aisle near where the young handsome clerk was standing.

"I haven't had a firkin in years."

"You haven't?" I thought you had," said her neighbor.

"No, I haven't, and I'd sure like to have one. Oh, here he comes now."

The young fellow approached and asked, "Yes, Ladies, can I help you this afternoon?"

"Well," said my friend, "I hope so. We were just commenting that I hadn't had a firkin in years."

The young man turned red, embarrassed at the apparent aggressiveness of a woman of her age.

"Well, ma'am, I'm afraid you're in the wrong place. We don't--"

"No, no," she interrupted. "There it is right there. Take a look at it. This is one of the nicest I've ever seen."

"Oh, you mean this cask. I'm sorry, I misunderstood."

"Yes, this wood container here. My mother had one and I had one when I first got married, and kept it for years, but I haven't seen one for a long time. My mother used to put butter and liquids in hers."

"Interesting," said the clerk.

"I'll take it," said my friend.

My Turn

Have you been to a doctor's office lately? If not, have you waited for a friend in the lobby of a hospital? Or in the lobby of a moderately-priced hotel? No? Well, maybe you've had occasion to drop by your lawyer's office, or your accountant's waiting room.

It doesn't really matter whether you're waiting at one of these or some other public place where magazines are spread around for the clients to read while they wait, the annoying result is the same: missing pages or portions thereof.

How satisfying it would be to lay this on the office personnel, but don't. It's the gentle public. They are there to fulfill their appointments. They often are smartly dressed, carry a straight face, with the chin held high throughout the sneaky ordeal.

Some will even smile or acknowledge your presence in a verbal way just before they are about to commit the petty indiscretion. They rip and tear--sometimes boldly, sometimes surreptitiously.

"Try coughing as you rip a page," one offender told me as she proudly boasted of her accomplishments. "It usually drowns out the ripping noise, but sometimes it doesn't," she said.

Maybe you need to use the bathroom, or pretend that you do, and take the magazine with you so that you can commit the crime without a witness. (Are some of the bathrooms equipped with hidden monitors? You never know.)

Then we have the culprits who tear just a small portion of a page. That doesn't take a loud cough, and if you hold the magazine sort of upward and close to your chest, it's difficult to know when the actual act is committed.

And then there is the client who has finished the appointment and is waiting to be picked up. When the driver arrives while she is in the middle of reading an article, she stands and walks hastily out the door. Forgot to leave the magazine, I presume. Really?

Just the other day in my doctor's office I was reading an account of a lady who had been married twice, and as she was walking down the aisle for the third time on a hot summer afternoon--the country church doors were left open because of the heat--a shaggy dog followed her and her brother who was giving her away. I couldn't wait to check "cont'd on page 34," to see how they handled getting rid of the dog. When I turned to page 34, some thoughtless person had ripped it out. Now I will never know whether the dog was meant to be a part of the ceremony or just loved humans and was curious.

While waiting at my dentist's office recently, a tempting tofu-banana cream pie recipe listed all the ingredients on page 25, but when you followed the "cont'd" instructions, the top half of the page had been removed, leaving only an ad for spinach casserole. I hate spinach.

One office visitor told me she has a collection of interesting articles she has copped from the various offices she has visited over the years. I suggested she try to publish them as "A Collection of Stolen Material." She didn't take kindly to the suggestion.

Now you might think that the people who are guilty of this kind of purloining are irresponsible, dishonest or not totally trustworthy. That may not be the case. They are ordinarily as honest as you and I. They are not afflicted with kleptomania. I haven't heard of any claiming to be victims who can't help themselves. I suspect that there are those out there, if pressed, who would be quick to tell you that they were abused as a child, often the standard excuse for aberrant behavior.

Recently I had occasion to be in another office and was reading an article on the six ways to becoming a better person. I read the first three, all excellent suggestions, but the last three neither I, nor anyone else who looks at that particular copy, will ever know how to apply. Some collector tore out the coupon for a free bottle of special tonic water.

I can't accost these people; I can't make a citizen's arrest, and I can't be a tattletale and report it to the receptionist. And if I did, the response would probably often be no more consoling than, "Oh, people do it all the time."

Well, isn't it about time that the public--at least those who read while waiting in offices--take a guilt test before leaving? After all, how would you like the success of your dinner party to be dependent upon knowing or not knowing the outcome of a special recipe because some inconsiderate person had ripped a portion of that page? And only because there was an article he had seen for "Ways to Increase Your Odds." For what?

If I could have my turn on this issue, I would ask that a placard be prominently placed in each of the offices. It would read:

"Our selection of magazines is here for your pleasure. Read what you can, copy all you wish, but please leave the pages intact."

A Best Time

While speaking before a group of senior citizens on the benefits of using the farmer's almanac for gardening, harvesting, and other activities around the homestead, one gentleman left his seat and the woman beside him. He moved to the front of the room, and raised his hand.

"Yes, sir. What is your question?"

"I would like to know if you can tell me the best time to file for divorce?"

I was non-plussed.

"Sorry, I can't. I am not versed in that subject at all."

"Thank you," he said, and then sat quietly throughout the rest of the lecture.

The following week I had occasion to be in the same meeting place to attend another person's lecture, and this gentleman was also there. When recess time approached I walked over to speak with him.

"You know something," I said, "I remember you from last week. You were the one who asked the question about the best time to file for divorce."

"You're right," he said, assuredly.

"Well, I just wondered why you would pose such a question while the lady you walked in with and were sitting beside--I assume it was your wife?"

"Yes, she is."

"And you would ask such a question as that with her in the audience?"

"Oh yes. You see, I didn't ask that question for myself; I am a happily married man. I asked it for my daughter, and she is not happily married."

Patches

After the services were over the preacher was talking to the young boy and noticed that the knees were out of his pants.

"Son, what happened? You don't have any patches there, just holes."

"Well, Sir," said the youngster, "I stay on my knees a lot praying."

"That's fine," said the preacher. "I'm glad to hear that you do,"

Several Sundays passed and the youngster again showed up, this time with the seat of his pants out.

"Hello there, good to see you again," said the preacher. "I notice that the seat of your pants is out. How come?"

"Preacher, it's like this: Lately I've been doing an awful lot of back-sliding."

If You Must, Do It Right

When he saw a young man going through gyrations and acting strange, he pulled over to the side of the road, got out of the car and walked over to the fellow.

"Young man," he said, "What in the world are you doing?"

"I'm trying to commit suicide," he said.

"Well, then, why in the world do you have that rope around your waist instead of your neck?"

"Well, I tied it around my neck and I couldn't breathe."

The Correct Name Helps

The wife had been demanding and controlling throughout their married life, telling her husband what to do, when, and where. A few weeks after he was buried she returned to the cemetery to visit his grave. After looking in all the areas, she was unable to locate his spot. She went to the office near the front gate of the cemetery for assistance.

"Sir," she said, "I've looked and looked and I can't find my husband's grave."

"Oh, I'm sure we can help you. I'll check the file. What is the husband's name?"

"His name is George Jackson," she said.

The fellow searched the files and said, "Ma'am, I'm sorry, but I don't have a George Jackson listed in the file. I have an Elizabeth Jackson."

"That's it, that's it," she said. "Everything is in my name."

Yell Loudly If You Must

A few years after their marriage, the husband came home earlier than expected one evening. The wife, in bed with another man, heard her husband coming in. She lay in the bed screaming at the top of her voice, "Help, Help, I'm being raped."

In the meantime the young fellow crawled out the window, but was later caught, and taken to jail.

He didn't have money for his bond, but it didn't take him long to amass it. And the way he acquired it was by beating the other inmates at Poker. He came up with the thousand dollar bail and was released, awaiting his trial date.

The Doctor's Posted Rate

ANSWERS: $1.00
ANY REQUIRING THOUGHT : $2.00
CORRECT ANSWERS: $4.00
DUMB LOOKS: Still free
Senior Citizens Discount available.

Essential Qualities

Several years ago a guest speaker at an insurance meeting said that every person in the insurance business should have two qualities: One, that it is desirable that they have either gray hair or be bald. This gives them a look of maturity. And second, and more important, it helps if they have hemorrhoids. This gives them a look of concern.

It Pays to Ask

While in a bookstore autographing two of our books about using the farmer's almanac for planting, harvesting, grafting, trimming, etc., my co-author also had his recent mystery novel on the table. A middle-aged woman stepped up, picked up the mystery and read the front and back covers.

"Did you write this?" she asked.

"Yes, I did," he replied.

"What inspired you to write it?"

He hesitated, and in jest, I said, "He just got out of jail."

Quick as a flash she came back, "Oh, you've written your memoirs?"

Tower Instructions

The new airport tower operator had been on the job only a short while when he received his first call from an incoming flight.

"Tower, Auracana Flight 407. Request landing instructions. Over."

"Tower to Auracana 407. Land East on Runway 9."

"Roger," said the pilot.

Within seconds Sureway 503 called in and requested landing instructions.

"Tower to Sureway 503. Land West on Runway 9."

"Tower, Sureway 503 again. Did you say land West on Runway 9?"

"Roger," said the Tower operator."

"But I thought I heard you just tell Auracana 407 to land East on Runway 9. Won't that be dangerous?"

Without a moment's hesitation, the Tower operator shot back, "Sorry, 503. Be careful."

The Census

The Census taker called on the home of a not too-well educated man with a wife and three children.

"Sir, I'm with the Census Bureau, and we are taking the decade census. Here are my credentials."

"I see," said the father. "And what do you want to know?"

"Well, sir, if you will, just answer a few questions for us."

"All right."

"Let's see here. I have your name, your wife's name, and it shows here that you have three children."

"That's right."

"I notice it has been more than ten years since the last one was born. Is that the caboose?"

"You bet your life," the father replied. "You see," he said, "Long ago I read in the almanac that every fourth child born in this world was Chinese, and I certainly don't want no child of mine that don't look like the rest of my children."

Shoplifting

The large superstore had run advertisements for several weeks announcing their opening date and the sales that would be on. I followed them closely, and on the appointed day stopped in on my way home from work. I purchased a cast iron frying pan, two pairs of sandals and began walking through the other aisles just to see what they had.

As I proceeded through the TV department I noticed a large wire basket near the center of the aisle. These types of baskets were scattered throughout the store, with various items in them, depending, of course, on the area. In this one basket were boxed Moulie graters, the kind that you use in grating cheese, carrots, and other food items.

I picked up one of the boxes, stepped over to the sales person near the cash register in the TV department.

"Can you take this here, sir, or do I have to go back to the Kitchenwares section?"

"No, problem," he said. "I can take it."

He took the box. I handed him the correct amount of money, and he punched the keys on the cash register. It locked. He couldn't get the drawer to open or the receipt to come out.

"That's all right," I said, "as long as you give me something to get me out of the store. I notice they have security all over the place, and especially at the exit doors. I have receipts for the other two items."

"Fine. I'll just stick this piece of tape on, and that should get you through," he responded.

I began walking toward the front entrance, and just as I was about to exit, I heard a voice. "Sir, hey. Sir, just a moment."

"Were you speaking to me?"

"Yes. What is that you have there? I notice that one item is not in a bag. May I see your ticket?"

"Sir, I don't have a ticket. I purchased this grater in the TV department, out of one of those wire baskets that are all over the place, and the register locked. He couldn't give me a receipt. I had the right change and he took that. He said that that piece of tape would get me through."

"Oh, is that right?" he said, with a smirk on his face. "And you say you got this in TV over there?"

"Yes. If you go back there I'll show you the man that sold it to me."

'Well, I'll tell you what you do," he said, "you come with me to Security."

"Officer, will you go to the TV department and let me show you the person I paid?"

At first I thought he was going to ignore my offer to demonstrate my honesty, but he took the box from the basket, held it in his right hand raised up near his shoulder and began walking back towards the TV department. As we were walking in the aisle running alongside the toiletry department a sales lady was standing behind the counter.

"What, another one?"

The security officer nodded his head but did not audibly respond, just continued toward the TV area, with me trailing behind.

"There is the gentleman that sold it to me, sir, right there."

"Yes, Officer. My register locked and I couldn't give him a receipt, but I put that piece of tape on it. That should have gotten him through."

The officer's only response was a grunt. He did not look toward me at all, just handed me the box and turned to leave, at which time I spoke.

"Officer, may I have your name, please?"

With a concerted effort, he thrust his left chest toward me so that I could see his badge.

"Thank you, Officer."

And with that he left the area. I left the store mad, and the closer I got to my home the madder I became. Nevertheless, I slept well during the night, returned to my job the next morning and mentioned it to a lawyer whose offices were across from mine.

After telling him of the incident he suggested I sue, and said that he would take the case at no expense to me unless there was a recovery. I chose not to pursue it any further because my court reporting schedule was heavy, and being as familiar with the legal system as I am, I knew it could become a drag, with continuances, unavailability of the officer to testify under oath, the act of coinciding all schedules with the lawyer's, my own, and the uncertainties of the day.

It was not until three days later that I picked up the paper and read that that same officer had been relieved of his duties for having been charged with conspiring with two "apparent customers" to remove items--in other words steal-- from this new store.

Only then was I made whole again, and able to laugh at the incident.

An Early Christmas (Maybe)

The stores were crowded with last-minute shoppers, and the fine jewelry store located on the second floor arcade of a tall downtown building was no exception.

As I walked through the ground floor arcade and was about to enter the elevator to go up to my 7th-floor office, there were many loud repetitive fire-cracker-type explosions in the ground floor arcade. Everyone began to scramble for cover. I punched the button for my floor, not knowing what had transpired, only that there was something wrong.

Once reaching my floor, I hurriedly stepped from the elevator, went to my office and tried to call the police but the line was constantly busy. Within minutes, a nicely dressed gentleman entered, carrying a brief case. He was short of breath and said he walked up the stairs, not trusting the elevators. He was sweating, and immediately asked if I had heard the explosion.

"Yes," I said, "I was just ready to enter the elevator when I heard all those firecrackers going off. What was it? Do You know?"

"No, but some lady said she heard that there were two men robbing the jewelry store on the 2nd floor arcade, and that they had set up some semi-elaborate wiring system on the ground arcade level and on the stairway leading to the 2nd floor arcade, near the jewelry store. She said she didn't know any more than that."

"Well, that was clever of them, if that is what happened. It would certainly distract the regular customers," I said.

"You're right. It takes guts to do something like that."

"Well," I said, "you seem mighty upset."

"I am, man. That's not funny. I thought it was rifle

shots, and that's not something you take a chance with this day and time."

"Just take your time; sit there until you're calmed down."

"Okay."

He sat in the outer office for another 20 or 30 minutes, then came in and thanked me for the kindness and left.

Later that day it was learned that Security was on duty, and had caught one of the two, but one of them had escaped. The one they caught was running from the building. When he was crossing the street, he stumbled and dropped a brief case. In so doing, the case snapped open and all the jewelry spilled onto the street. The other one they hadn't captured as of late afternoon.

It wasn't until I was reading the next morning's paper, saw the headlines and looked at the picture of the two men, that I realized the man I had befriended was the very one I had unknowingly helped evade the law--at least for awhile.

A Lick and a Promise

"Now, boys, this afternoon I want you to straighten up that hay loft," my father said. "And don't give it just a lick and a promise."

I don't know where the expression originated, but it was one used often in the area of the state of North Carolina where I was born.

A "lick and a promise" meant giving the job a quick one-two, with the promise to do it right or better the next time.

My youngest brother, only four at the time, and although having never had the expression used on him, had heard my father use it numerous times. He was in the yard one afternoon when my father was getting ready to punish an older brother for something he had done that he should not have.

He watched as my father walked over to the tree, broke off a switch and headed toward my older brother.

"Daddy," he cried out, "don't whip him, don't whip him. Just give him a 'lick and a promise.'"

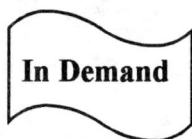

In Demand

One of the more popular preachers was asked just what he attributed his great demand for speaking.

"Well, I will tell you how it is," he said. "I always say a silent prayer before every sermon, and it goes like this: 'Dear Lord, please fill my mouth with worthwhile stuff, but nudge me when I've said enough.'"

It's a Two-way Street

All times are political times. There are no exceptions. While working as a court reporter, I had occasion to report a speaker who spoke of both Democrats and Republicans. He said:

"Democrats buy and read books that have been banned someplace, but Republicans form Censorship Committees and read them as a group.

"Republicans consume three-fourths of the rutabagas consumed in this country, and the balance is destroyed.

"Republicans often wear hats and almost always clean their paint brushes.

"Democrats give their worn-out clothes to people who are less fortunate than they. Republicans wear theirs.

"Republicans employ exterminators, but Democrats step on the bugs.

"Democrats name their children after currently popular entertainment and sports figures, and Republican children are named after their grandparents, aunts and uncles, or parents, according to where the money is.

"Republicans tend to keep their shades drawn although there is little reason to. Democrats ought to but don't.

"Republicans read the financial pages of the newspapers. Democrats put them in the bottom of the bird cage.

"Most of the stuff along the road is thrown out of car windows by Democrats.

"Republicans raise dahlias, Dalmatians and eyebrows. Democrats raise Airedales, kids and taxes.

"Democrats eat the fish they catch; Republicans put them on the wall.

"Republican boys date Democrat girls. They will

155

marry Republican girls, but think they are entitled to a little fun first.

"Democrats make plans and then do something else, but Republicans follow the plans their grandfathers made.

"Republicans sleep in twin beds, and that's why there are more Democrats."

Good-bye American Rose

No one can deny the evidence that there is heavy traffic and a lot of road-building going on throughout our country. It is becoming more hectic every day. In fact, if it continues, we might want to designate the "CLOVERleaf" as our National flower.

Just about everyone overeats at one time or another, and often some feel guilty about it, but Victor Buono has penned this clever poem which probably speaks for many:

Eating

O Lord my soul is ripped with riot,
Incited by my wicked diet.
We are what we eat, said a wise old man.
Lord if that's true, I'm a garbage can.
I want to rise on judgment day that's plain
But at my present weight, I'd need a crane.
Lord give me strength that I may not fall
In the clutches of cholesterol.
Let my flesh with carrot curls be sated
That my soul may be polyunsaturated.
Lord make me strong that I may bear witness
To the President's Council on physical fitness.
About oleomargarine I'll never mutter,
For the road to Hell is paved with butter.
And cream is wicked and cake is awful
And Satan is hiding in every waffle.
Mephistopheles lurks in provolone
The devil is in each slice of baloney.
    Beelzebub is a chocolate drop
    And Lucifer is a lollypop.
    Give me this day my daily slice,
    But cut it thin and toast it twice.
    I beg you on my dimpled knees,
    Deliver me from JuJuBees.
    And when my time of trial is done,
    And my war with malted milk is won,
    Let me be up there with the saints in heaven

In a shining robe, size thirty-seven.
I can do it Lord if you'll show to me
The good in greens and celery,
And the wickedness that is mayonnaise,
And the evil that is hollandaise,
And pasta a la Milanaise,
And potatoes a la Lyonaise,
And deep fried chicken from the south.
       Lord if you love me. . .shut my mouth.

Heavenly Bliss

They told me old age
was heavenly bliss
I wanted to believe them
and see what I'd missed
But now that it's here
and in full swing
They certainly were wrong
Or I missed a fling

Stepchildren

A friend sent me this story about the man in his late 30s who had never been married. The reason, it was said, is that he just detested children, couldn't tolerate kids.

He eventually did marry, however, and married a widow with three children. People said it would never last, not with the kids involved.

A couple of months passed and one of the neighbors saw one of the boys out in the front yard and asked him, "Son, how is that new dad of yours?"

And the young boy said, "Oh, he's just fine."

"What do you mean?" inquired the neighbor.

"Well, he gives us candy, and we get to go for rides, and we go swimming once a week. He's really a great dad."

"Where do you go swimming?" the neighbor asked.

"Oh, down at the ocean, and he takes us out about a mile and lets us swim back."

"Really?"

"Oh, yes. He's just a super dad."

"Well, isn't that kind of rough, swimming back from that far out?"

"No, it's not bad, not once we get out of the sack."

Talented

The young man and girl had been going together for several months, and he was getting close to proposing.

"Tell me, Sweetheart, I know that your mother knows a lot about me, and to some extent your father, but do they know all the good?"

"Like what?"

"Well, I'm not a bad guy; you'll have to admit. Let's face it; right?"

"Well, I've told them both about your gambling and drinking."

"What about my poetry? Have you told them that I am a writer and that I write a lot of poetry?"

"No, I haven't. I couldn't tell them everything at once."

Wedding Dictionary (Revised Edition)

Marriage Contract:	The "I Do" binder
Preacher:	Peacemaker
Bride:	The victorious
Groomsmen:	They Also Ran
Flower Girl:	Fragrant bearers
Ushers:	Well-dressed seaters
Groomsmen:	Friendly pallbearers
Maid of Honor:	Chief female supporter
The Bridesmaids:	The bride's "Her'em"
Rehearsal Dinner:	The Groom's family payoff
Wedding Gown:	Smocked alleged virginity
Invitations:	Solicitation brochures
Tuxedoes:	Foreign dress
Nosegay:	Fragrant decoy
Wrist Bouquets:	Surplus flowers
Ring Bearer:	Debt carrier

The Rooster

Just as I opened this book with a story about a dear friend and her experience with Reuben, the parrot, on the Greyhound bus, I shall now close with another story about her.

She is indeed a fowl lover. On one occasion she took her Auracana rooster and three hens, put them in a special made pen, and put the pen in her van. She left Charlotte with her driver early in the morning for Miami. It was a long day and she arrived late in the night.

The Miami area in which she lives is upscale, with strict zoning and restrictions. No live poultry is allowed. Upon her late arrival, and not wanting to drive farther down to Homestead to leave them with her farm friend, she called it a day at her place in Miami.

She removed the pen and placed it in her utility house. And because they had been cooped up nearly 14 hours, she opened the crate door, so they would have the run of the utility house.

It was not until the next morning when she was out taking her constitutional walk and ran into a neighbor doing likewise, that she learned the latest.

"Oh, good morning," said the neighbor. "How nice to have you back."

"Good morning," my friend said. "It's good to be back."

They chatted briefly and then the neighbor asked, "Did you hear something that sounded like a rooster crowing early this morning?"

"A rooster crowing? In this neighborhood?"

My friend continued her walk. Immediately after

returning and having breakfast, she clandestinely loaded her "passengers" in the van, drove farther south and delivered them to her farmer friend for safe-keeping during the winter.

So you see, neighborhoods are neighborhoods, some more upscale than others. But certainly the rooster would have been insulted had he heard: "A rooster crowing? In this neighborhood?"

My deep Appreciation to the following:

Martha Hendricks
Gina Maretta
Maddalena Cerri
"Duck" Boone
Anne and Wayne Williams
Dr. Bill Bell
Jim Watson
Carrie Jane McGarey
Mildred Gilley
Edith Keys
Jack Ward
David Whorf
Dr. John McCormack
Johnnie Thomas
Lila Rae Yawn

And to a special group for a special reason:

Sally Cochran
Dick Mowers
Dick and Millie Heiling
Al and Betty Marshall
Joe and Roberta Sweeney
Opal Looke
Marilyn Barber
Florine Varner
Charlie Barnes
Phyllis Gainey
Gertrude Lynch

Carol Colston
Mary Louise Gilman
Virginia Rankin
Vivien Spitz
Mae Glassbrenner
Robert Wright
David Daily
Sam Fitz-Henley
Charlie Wall
Lollie Hammond
Richard and Norma Smith

And with a double tribute to Rachel Lerschen, a storyteller without parallel.

Acknowledgments

I gratefully acknowledge the publications shown below who were kind enough to publish some of my work when the stories, jokes, poetry and essays were originally written and now comprise portions of this book of humor.

Alive
Book of American Traditions
Capper's
Christian Single
Country America
Country Woman
Down Memory Lane
Elder Update
Farm and Ranch
North Carolina Farm Bureau
Our Family
Progressive Farmer
Saturday Evening Post